ε1

The Women's Press Ltd
34 Great Sutton Street, London EC1V 0DX

Jacklyn Cock is a Senior Lecturer in the Department of Sociology at the University of the Witwatersrand, Johannesburg. From an Eastern Cape family herself, she conducted this research while lecturing at Rhodes University, Grahamstown. She holds degrees in Political Science, History and Sociology.

Jacklyn Cock

Maids and Madams

Domestic Workers under
Apartheid

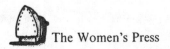 The Women's Press

This revised edition first published by The Women's Press Limited 1989
A member of the Namara Group
34 Great Sutton Street, London EC1V 0DX

Maids and Madams was first published in South Africa by
Ravan Press Ltd, 1980

British Library Cataloguing in Publication Data
Cock, Jacklyn
    Maids and madams: domestic workers under apartheid.
    1. South Africa. Women. Domestic service
    I. Title
    640'.46'088042

    ISBN 0-7043- 4165-4

Typeset by AKM Associates (UK) Ltd, Southall, London
Printed and bound in Great Britain by
Hazell, Watson & Viney Limited, Aylesbury, Bucks

To Mother, Kathie, Margaret and Bill

The Making of a Servant

I can no longer ask how it feels
To be choked by a yoke-rope
Because I have seen it for myself in the chained ox.
The blindness has left my eyes. I have become aware,
I have seen the making of a servant
In the young yoke-ox.

He was sleek, lovely, born for freedom,
Not asking anything from any one, simply
   priding himself on being a young ox.
Someone said: Let him be caught and
   trained and broken in,
Going about it as if he meant to help him.
I have seen the making of a servant
In the young yoke-ox.

He tried to resist, fighting for his freedom.
He was surrounded, fenced in with wisdom and experience.
They overcame him by trickery: 'He must be trained.'
A good piece of rationalisation can camouflage evil.
I have seen the making of a servant
In the young yoke-ox.

He was bound with ropes that cut into his head,
He was bullied, kicked, now and again petted,
But their aim was the same: to put a yoke on him.
Being trained in one's own interests is for the privileged.
I have seen the making of a servant
In the young yoke-ox.

The last stage. The yoke is set on him.
They tie the halter round his neck, slightly choking him.
They say the job's done, he'll be put out to work with
    the others
To obey the will of his owner and taskmaster.
I have seen the making of a servant
In the young yoke-ox.

He kicks out, trying to break away.
They speak with their whips. He turns backwards
Doing his best to resist but then they say: 'Hit him.'
A prisoner is a coward's plaything.
I have seen the making of a servant
In the young yoke-ox.

Though he stumbled and fell, he was bitten on the tail.
Sometimes I saw him raking at his yoke-mate
With his horns — his friend of a minute, his blood-brother.
The suffering under the yoke makes for bad blood.
I have seen the making of a servant
In the young yoke-ox.

The sky seemed black as soft rain fell.
I looked at his hump, it was red,
Dripping blood, the mark of resistance.
He yearns for his home, where he was free.
I have seen the making of a servant
In the young yoke-ox.

Stockstill, tired, there was no sympathy.
He bellowed notes of bitterness.
They loosened his halter a little — to let him breathe,
They tightened it again, snatching back his breath.
I have seen the making of a servant
In the young yoke-ox.

I saw him later, broken, trained,
Pulling a double-shared plough through deep soil,
Serving, struggling for breath, in pain.
To be driven is death. Life is doing things for yourself.
I have seen the making of a servant
In the young yoke-ox.

I saw him climb the steepest of roads.
He carried heavy loads, staggering —
The mud of sweat which wins profit for another.
The savour of working is a share in the harvest.
I have seen the making of a servant
In the young yoke-ox.

I saw him hungry with toil and sweat,
Eyes all tears, spirit crushed,
No longer able to resist. He was tame.
Hope lies in action aimed at freedom.
I have seen the making of a servant
In the young yoke-ox.

The Making of a Servant and other Poems by J.J.R. Jolobe.
Translated from Xhosa by Robert Kavanagh and Z.S. Qangule
(*Ophir*, Ravan Press, Johannesburg, 1974)

Contents

Preface

This book is based on research done in the Eastern Cape area of South Africa in 1978 and 1979. That research was undertaken in the belief that sociologists in South Africa have a particular obligation to record the injustice and exploitation that surround us and of which we are too often a contributing part. If the book has any value it is that it allows the voices of domestic workers to be heard. These voices need, however, to be located in terms of the social structures and historical processes which have silenced them for so long. A danger in this kind of sociological analysis is that the living nature of the feelings, ideas and hopes of the people studied becomes frozen and obscured in academic jargon and long computer sheets covered with endless statistics. I have tried to avoid this.

This British edition of *Maids and Madams* includes five chapters which originally appeared in a longer, more academic book of the same title that was published in South Africa by Ravan Press in 1980. These chapters are included because they are still relevant to the experiential meaning of domestic service as an institution. Chapters One and Seven have been specially written for this edition.

Maids and Madams gives a tentative and exploratory account of an institution which has been an essential part of the white South African way of life for generations. Perhaps the Eastern Cape, on which the research was focused, is South Africa's 'Deep South', but there is a sense in which the institution of domestic service itself constitutes apartheid's Deep South in that it is still the crudest, and most hidden, expression of inequality in this society.

In the eight intervening years since this material was first published conditions *have* changed. For instance, wages have risen. A 1986 study estimated that the average wage of black workers in Grahamstown is the equivalent of £10.70 a month, as against an estimated subsistence level of £60 per month per worker. This is higher than the wages reported in this book. However, what is undeniable is that the wages of black workers generally and domestic workers specifically are still abysmally low. Furthermore it is debatable to what extent this £10.70 represents an increase in real terms given that South Africa has had an inflation rate of 18 per cent per annum for some time now.

This book is an indictment of the liberal mentality which asserts the humanity of Africans, only to deny the human needs and feelings of African servants. It would not have been completed without the support and assistance of several friends. I would like to acknowledge my debt to five people especially: first, my field worker, Nobengazi Mary Kota, whose skill and sensitivity elicited a remarkable degree of trust from the domestic workers she interviewed. Second, Professor Edward Higgins, who supervised the research on which this book is based. I am indebted to him for his help especially during the period of field work, and for his openness to opinions and perspectives which he does not share. I am extremely grateful to Dorothy Driver and Nick Visser who edited the manuscript and whose suggestions have made the text far more readable than it would otherwise have been. Lastly, I am especially indebted to Kathleen Satchwell whose encouragement and incisive criticism have been invaluable.

I should like also to acknowledge the work of Ros de Lanerolle, Alison Mansbridge and Daphne Tagg on this new edition. Finally I am indebted to the domestic workers and their employers who gave up their time to be interviewed, and who spoke with such honesty and vividness about their lives. I have learned a great deal from them.

Johannesburg, July 1988

Maids and Madams

Domestic Workers under Apartheid

1 Introduction

Wife and servant are the same, but only differ
in the name.
Lady Chudleigh

The situation of black and white women in South
Africa presents a challenge to any oversimplified feminist notion of
'sisterhood'. That challenge is sharpest in the institution of domestic
service where the wages paid and the hours of work exacted by white
'madams' from their black 'maids' suggest a measure of oppression of
women by women.

In South Africa most white households employ servants. Poverty,
labour controls and a lack of employment alternatives combine to
'trap' many African women in domestic service. They are trapped in a
condition of immobility within which they are subject to intense
oppression. Such oppression is evident in their low wages and long
working hours and in the demeaning treatment of them by the white
women who are their employers. ('She does not see me as a woman.
She looks down on me.') This oppression is expressed in many
domestic servants' sense of being slaves, of leading wasted lives which
they are powerless to change. ('I have been a slave all my life.' 'We are
slaves in our own country.') Other Africans also experience their
working lives as a form of slavery. This is because Africans in South
Africa are one of the most regimented labour forces in the contemporary world. In this context feminist theory has to be sensitive to the
complex inter-relation of race, gender and class. The intersection of
these three lines of oppression in the situation of black women in South
Africa raises important questions regarding both the limits and the
possibilities of feminist struggle. Feminists here are forced 'to
recognise that white women stand in a power relation as oppressors of
black women'. (Carby, 1982: 214.)

It was as a feminist that I was first drawn to examine the institution of domestic service, as the social space within which black and white women most frequently encounter each other. Writing the Preface before the publication of my research findings in September 1979, I wrote: 'The publication of *Maids and Madams* may evoke controversy. Indeed while writing it, I have felt akin to Marx's worker, "like someone who has brought his own hide to market and now has nothing to expect but a tanning".' (Cock, 1980: 2.) While I escaped a 'tanning', the publication did provoke a stream of abusive phone-calls: most of these were from men threatening physical abuse of various kinds from rape to murder; sometimes the calls were silent or involved the sound of a clock ticking or maniacal laughter. They had reached an average level of five a day, when there was a dynamite attack on my home. (See Appendix 1.) The incident was reported in the local newspaper as follows:

> Street lights in Cross Street, Grahamstown, went out
> mysteriously just before a 20-centimetre-long pack of dynamite
> sticks was hurled through a front window of the home of Rhodes
> University lecturer, Ms Jacklyn Cock, on Thursday night. The
> dynamite landed in the dining room, where she was having a late
> supper with two friends. It failed to explode but smouldered for
> about half an hour while police explosives experts worked at
> removing it. (*Eastern Province Herald*, 6.12.1980.)

If I had known the extent of the anger my research would provoke I doubt very much that I would have found the courage to complete it.

I still believe that the research is significant, because the institution of domestic service has a peculiar importance in South African society. In the first place it constitutes a significant source of employment for almost one million black women. This fact is highly anomalous given South Africa's level of industrial development.

Katzman, in his analysis of domestic service in the USA between 1870 and 1920, characterises it as a 'non-industrial' rather than a 'pre-industrial' occupation. (Katzman, 1978: 146.) The occupation has a number of characteristics which define the difference between domestic servants and other wage workers. Other wage workers sell their labour power as a commodity for a definite period of time in exchange for a money wage. Work relationships are impersonal and involve a clear separation between workplace and home, in both temporal and spatial terms. The domestic servant by contrast frequently works irregular hours; she receives part of her payment 'in kind' and the 'live-in' domestic servant is accommodated at the work-place. Employer control often extends into the servant's 'private life' – for example the regulation of visitors and the inspection of the servant's rooms and goods. The highly personalised nature of the servant's relationship with her employer and the low level of speciali-sation in domestic roles are both anomalous in a modern industrial society moving towards specialised and impersonal work relationships. Second, domestic workers play a crucial role in the reproduction of 'labour power', the capacity to work. This includes not only physical maintenance (through cooking and cleaning), but also ideological maintenance. Often the institution of domestic service is the only significant inter-racial contact whites experience, and they experience the relationship in extremely asymmetrical terms. Many white South African children are socialised into the dominant ideological order and learn the attitudes and styles of racial domination from relation-ships with servants, especially 'nannies'. The converse is equally true in that many black children experience the inequality of apartheid and the anger it generates through some experience of domestic service. For example, Steve Biko first became politicised through observing the exploitation to which his mother was subject as a domestic worker. Many blacks report experiences of fractured and deprived childhoods because of this institution. One of the accused in the current Delmas trial, now in its second year, the general secretary of the United Democratic Front, Popo Molefe, described in court how he:

> . . . grew up with his aunt and uncle under 'conditions of considerable poverty'. The position was aggravated by the death of his uncle in 1960. His aunt was forced to work as a domestic and he was left in the care of her daughter. 'I learnt to fend for myself at an early age' he told the judge. (*The Star*, 8.8.1987.)

Theophilus Mzukwa, aged twenty-six, was convicted of terrorism in the African National Congress trial in Cape Town in 1987. He described how he came to his decision that 'it was far better to fight for freedom and perhaps die in the process, than live like a slave':

> Mzukwa described how his mother, who was working for R60 (£20) per month as a domestic servant, had 'more time for the children of her white employer than she had for us'. (*Weekly Mail*, 12.6.1987.)

This points to one of the most intense sources of strain experienced by domestic workers. Many of the women interviewed reported that they had to look after two families and neglect their own in the process. On the whole they are markedly powerless to alter their situation. Lack of educational opportunities and employment alternatives, coupled with legislation restricting the movement of black workers, all combine to 'trap' black women in domestic service. The predominant response obtained from the 225 domestic workers interviewed in this study was a sense of being trapped; of having no alternatives; of living out an infinite series of daily frustrations, indignities and denials.

It is suggested in the following four chapters that as an occupational group domestic workers are subject to a level of 'ultra-exploitation'. They are denied a negotiated wage, reasonable working hours, family and social life. They are also denied favourable working conditions, respectful treatment and any acknowledgement of the dignity of their labour, as well as specific legal protection and effective bargaining power. These chapters attempt to penetrate the veiled and hidden abode of reproduction – the household – and document these denials at an experiential level.

Domestic workers and their employers are not free and equal participants in interaction. Their interaction is shaped and coloured by the structures which control the distribution of power and resources in South African society. These structures define the relationship between whites and blacks as:

> . . . a master-servant relationship in all spheres, enforced through a variety of effective controls and sanctions. It is a system in which the Africans are forced to work for the whites at bare subsistence wages (perhaps not even that), deprived of all basic rights to assert their interests freely and legally, and subject to some of the most draconian and tyrannical labour controls ever developed in modern industry. The enormous power and prosperity of the whites in South Africa is thus based on the systematic exploitation of African labour. (Johnstone, 1970: 136.)

In a very real sense the institution of domestic service is a microcosm of the exploitation and inequality on which the entire social order is based.

This social order creates and maintains the 'ultra-exploitability' of domestic workers. Their powerlessness and vulnerability derive from the oppression to which both blacks and women are subject in South Africa. This oppression is institutionalised to a degree that warrants discussion in terms of two systems: one of racial domination and one of sexual domination.

Various measures of racial domination serve to maintain blacks in a subordinate position. The conquest of blacks and appropriation of their land is the basis of this subordination. In terms of the Native Land Acts of 1913 and 1936, 87 per cent of the territory of South Africa is defined as 'white areas' in which Africans are not allowed to purchase or otherwise acquire land. This separation of blacks from the means of production constituted a form of economic compulsion forcing them into providing cheap labour for the white owners. This labour is controlled through a migrant labour system which operates through a complex body of legal and administrative measures.

The fulcrum of this system used to be the 'pass laws' or system of influx control. The abolition of this system in July 1986 was presented as a major reform by the Botha government. However, the new identity documents and policy of 'orderly urbanisation' inscribed in apartheid laws such as the Group Areas Act, the Land Acts, the Trespass Act and the Prevention of Illegal Squatting Act, together operate to severely restrict freedom of movement among the black population. Although the controls are more subtle and indirect, the right to be in a 'white' industrial centre or farm is largely tied to the availability of jobs and housing. The effect is to divide the black population between those legally in 'white' urban areas who have access to the capitalist core, and those excluded in the homelands or 'Bantustans'. The 'homelands' thus function both as labour reservoirs for the centres of capital accumulation and as 'dumping grounds' for surplus labour. (Walker and Platzky, 1985.)

These controls operate very coercively upon African women and bind domestic workers especially tightly. All domestic workers have to be registered. Those who are migrants on one-year contracts may have their contract renewed annually as long as they remain in the same job. As with other African migrants, changing jobs requires that the new employer makes a special application to a local administration board, proving that no African local labour is available. Thus the effect of this legislation is to impose an embargo on the entry of unskilled African women into 'white' urban areas, and to bind domestic workers to their present employers. Losing their job could well mean forced removal to the teeming rural slums of the 'homelands'.

Unlike other African workers, domestic workers are situated in a legal vacuum within this coercive structure. They are not protected by any legislation; there are no laws stipulating the minimum wages, hours of work or other conditions of service. The lack of disability and unemployment insurance, maternity benefits and paid sick leave means that they are an extremely insecure group of workers. They are vulnerable to instant dismissal by their employers who often fail to observe the common law provisions.

> No matter if I work here for one hundred years I can be
> dismissed for breaking a cup and get nothing. Not even a thank
> you.

Dismissal increasingly means endorsement out of an urban area or from a white-owned farm to the homelands.

It is in the homelands that the majority (57 per cent) of African women are trapped by laws prohibiting their movement to urban areas in 'white' South Africa. (Simkins, 1983: 57.) Lack of employment opportunities means some women surviving by seasonal work on white-owned farms for wages as low as 20 pence a day. For others, such as Rose living in the homeland of Lebowa, land shortage means being caught in a vicious circle of poverty.

> Now we have no ploughing fields. We are dying of hunger. Once
> the agricultural officers called us together to teach us how to
> farm, but this never happened again. They told us to buy
> fertilizer but it cost £2 or more a bag, and us starving people, we
> have no money. (Lawton, 1985: 99.)

But even in these desperate circumstances an incredible level of resourcefulness, energy and determination emerges from women such as Ma Dlomo Lugogo, from Transkei, who was struck by lightning but survived by selling bundles of thatching grass at £7 a hundred. (Lawton, 1985: 102.)

By comparison the African women in the urban areas of 'white' South Africa with legal rights to seek employment and obtain accommodation are fortunate. However, even among this group unemployment is high and brings hardships. As one woman commented: 'Unemployment brings three difficulties, sickness, starvation and staying without clothes.' (Barrett *et al.*, 1985: 92.) Unemployment is rising sharply in South Africa and many African women survive by exercising their initiative in 'informal sector' activities such as hawking, brewing or childminding, in a stressful and precarious existence.

Stress is also a constant factor in the lives of many African women wage-workers. Poverty and the massive disorganisation of African family life in contemporary South Africa lie behind the increase in the employment of black women generally in recent years. This increase was especially dramatic between 1973 and 1981 when there was a 51.7 per cent increase in the number of black women employed. (Favis, 1983: 5.) These women are mainly located in the service and agricultural sectors in the least skilled, lowest paid and most insecure jobs. In 1982 the percentage distribution of African women in the economy was as follows: 11 per cent of employed African women were in the professional sector (mainly nursing and teaching which accounted for 95 per cent of African women employed in this sector); 3 per cent in the clerical sector; 5 per cent in the sales sector; 17 per cent in agricultural production; 13 per cent in manufacturing; and 50 per cent in services (including domestic service). (Favis, 1983: 7.)

Although the female percentage of the industrial workforce is still relatively small, the absolute number of women involved in manufacturing has increased dramatically. However, the majority of women are confined to the production of food, clothing and textiles. This reflects the sexual division of labour generally as women's traditional activities in the household have been transferred to the factory. Food, clothing and textiles are labour-intensive sectors where wages are particularly low. There is only one industry where women constitute the majority of the black workforce, namely clothing, where 83 per cent of those employed are black women. In 1981 the average monthly wage for Africans employed in the clothing industry was £40. Evidence of extremely low wages in the 1980s also comes from a national survey of over 800 African women employed in the clothing industry and retail trade – the majority earned £100 or less a month. (Cock *et al.*, 1983: 26.) Similarly the majority (78 per cent) of a sample of 992 black women employed in factories in the Durban area earned £70 or less a month. (Meer, 1975.)

It is thus clear that while African women's participation in wage labour in South Africa has increased noticeably in recent years, they are confined to a narrow range of occupations which reflect both ideological definitions of 'women's work', and the fact of black women being a preferred source of labour because they are cheaper.

Their working conditions are often appalling. Nomvula who works the night shift as an office cleaner describes how she has to sleep on the chilly bare floor of her changing room when she finishes work at 3.30 a.m.:

> We sleep in our changing rooms. The place is sometimes very cold. There's no carpet on the floor – only tiles. You just take cardboard boxes and sleep on the floor. Sometimes you sit in the chair and you sleep sitting like this. (Lawton, 1985: 21.)

Nomvula cannot leave for her Soweto home when she finishes her shift because there is no transport available. It is not altogether safe when she does leave at 5.30 a.m. but she has to do so in order to get home in time to prepare breakfast for her children. By 2 p.m. she is back on the bus for the first leg of her journey to begin work four hours later.

Clearly this work pattern has a deleterious effect on health. A small survey of night cleaners found that a quarter of the women interviewed got only two or three hours sleep a day. All of these women complained of stomach problems, headaches and high blood pressure (Arenson and Molzen, 1983):

> This job makes me sick. You've got sore eyes and you've got headaches all the time because you don't sleep full hours. Some women take snuff to keep themselves awake at work. We're taking tablets . . . so that we don't sleep. Because you can't work when you are feeling sleepy. The tablets aren't healthy, but what can we do because we've got headaches and sore feet from standing all night, and backache from scrubbing – going up and down like that. And you've got tension, you feel dizzy, you don't know how you are. That's why you take tablets. Sometimes we just feel like leaving. But we've got no choice. If we could get easier jobs, we'd do it. But there's no work in South Africa. We must pay rent, we must feed our children. That's why we do night shift. (Lawton, 1985: 23.)

This absence of choice is a dominant theme. Many of the women interviewed in recent studies expressed their sense of being trapped workers whose vulnerability gives them no option but to acquiesce to low wages and appalling working conditions. The level of aspiration expressed by one 42-year-old African woman in Soweto reflects this: 'I am looking for work. I would like to work under the West Rand Board collecting rubbish in the streets.' (Barrett *et al.*, 1985: 90.)

Low wages, poor working conditions and long hours are not the only problems black women in South Africa contend with. Sexual harassment or 'love abuse', varying from jokes and insults to acts of rape and jobs in exchange for sex, appear to be common (Bird, 1985: 89):

> The position of women workers is too heavy, with many things: say you are a woman and you are looking for a job. When you reach a factory, you find the *induna* there and you ask him. If you like the job the *induna* will tell you that you must sleep with him before you get the job. And you've got no choice. You want to work and your children are starving in Soweto. So, some women sleep with those men. (Lawton, 1985: 26.)

It has been suggested that the recent repeal of the Immorality Act prohibiting sexual intercourse between members of different racial groups will increase the vulnerability of black women workers to sexual harassment.

Another major source of strain in these women's lives is the tension between their roles as mothers and as workers. Full-time motherhood is impossible for many urban African women compelled to support themselves and their dependants, or to supplement their husbands' low earnings. A national survey of over 800 African women workers found that 66 per cent were mothers of pre-school children. (Cock *et al.*, 1983: 17.) Economic necessity propelled most of these women into wage labour:

> It's hard. I feel it's important that a mother look after her own children. Money shouldn't come first. But what can we do? (Cock *et al.*, 1983: 44.)

Frequently such women are coerced into wage labour while their children are very young. According to a social worker, 'most African mothers have to go back to work when their children are less than three months old. The children are not breastfed and can suffer from malnutrition.' (Cock *et al.*, 1983: 42.) In a national study almost a quarter (20 per cent) of the mothers interviewed went back to work when their last child was less than two months old; 62 per cent did so when their last child was one year or younger, and over half

(52 per cent) went back when their last child was six months old or younger.

The inadequacy of creches and neglect of African child-care arrangements by the state is a major source of strain in these women's lives. In a national study almost 40 per cent of the women are leaving their children in the care of adult relatives, particularly grandmothers. The tightening up of controls and consequent fracturing of the African family in recent years often mean young children being sent away to remote rural areas. The pain this involves emerges from the informant who said:

> My child does not remember that I am her mother. She doesn't love me too much and this is difficult for me. (Lawton, 1985: 77.)

This pain is amplified for the black women employed as nannies to care for the children of their employers and who are separated from their own children in the process:

> My madam she does nothing, but she can live in this nice house and have fat children. My children are hungry. (Barrett *et al.*, 1985:34.)

> We leave our children early in the morning to look after other women's families and still they don't appreciate us.

In their daily struggle for survival, children are an important source of joy and meaning to many African women. As one informant expressed it:

> Even if it is expensive, children are making us happy. (Malcolm, 1983: 57.)

However, child-care is one component of the 'dual shift', the double load of work both inside and outside the home, which African women workers experience. The outcome is a continual drain of resources and energy, born of tension, conflict and sheer overwork.

This overwork is a constant feature of the experience of working-class women in other cultural and historical contexts. However, among African women this is compounded by legislation restricting housing for different racial groups to different areas, which means extra hours each day spent travelling long distances between home and the workplace. Also all recent research reports that men's involvement in domestic work is virtually non-existent among the African working class. The sexual division of labour within the home defines cooking, shopping, cleaning and child-care very rigidly as 'women's work'. However, in the urban working-class context, other women members of the household provide a valuable support network.

Such female support networks do 'provide a startling contrast to the isolated position of women in the Euro-American nuclear family structure'. (Carby, 1982: 231.) Carby makes the cogent point that 'in concentrating solely upon the isolated position of white women in the Western nuclear family structure, feminist theory has necessarily neglected the very strong female support networks that exist in many black sex/gender systems'. (Carby, 1982: 230.) In the South African context these female support networks function as strategies of survival; they are of inestimable value to the women coping with the strain of their dual roles of mothers and workers. A peculiarly South African twist comes from the fact that it is sometimes the black women employed as domestic servants who dilute the isolation of the white housewife. Some elderly employers living alone seem very dependent on their domestic servants for company. One said plaintively that she feels 'very alone in the world' when her servant goes off duty in the evenings.

This is an example of a much wider process whereby white women are able to divest themselves of a considerable part of domestic work and responsibilities – especially the care of young children – through the employment of domestic workers. Thus cheap black domestic labour is the instrument whereby many white women are freed from many of the oppressive and onerous aspects of the system of sexual domination.

This illustrates what Olive Schreiner termed 'female parasitism'. She speaks of women 'clad in fine raiment, the work of other's fingers, waited on and tended by the labour of others, fed on luxurious viands, the result of other's toil', seeking 'by dissipation and amusements to fill up the inordinate blank left by the lack of productive activity'. (Schreiner, 1911: 81.) Schreiner recognised that the basis of female parasitism was exploitation:

> Behind the phenomenon of female parasitism has always lain another and yet larger social phenomenon; it has invariably been preceded . . . by the subjugation of large bodies of other human creatures, either as slaves, subject races, or classes; and as the

result of the excessive labours of those classes there has always been an accumulation of unearned wealth in the hands of the dominant class or race . . . Without slaves or subject classes to perform the crude, physical labours of life and produce superfluous wealth, the parasitism of the female would in the past have been an impossibility. (Schreiner, 1911: 98.)

Thus Schreiner showed that exploitation has a price: sexist definitions of femininity are more coercive and restricting for women of the dominant class. This is symbolised in the small, smooth, unused, lily-white hands and long unbroken fingernails which indicate upper-class membership, the hands of those who are, as Mary Wollstonecraft expressed it, 'reduced to the status of birds confined to their cages with nothing to do but plume themselves and stalk with mock majesty from perch to perch'. (Gavron, 1973: 21.)

All women in South Africa are subjected to a sexist and patriarchal ideology which defines women as secondary, inferior and dependent. There are several points of similarity between racism and sexism. Both are justificatory ideologies, serving to legitimise a system of domination. They have been used to justify both economic exploitation and the denial of political rights. In terms of content there is a great deal of similarity between the conception of the female in a sexist ideology and the Sambo myth which defines blacks as irresponsible, child-like and incompetent. This conception commonly includes qualities such as passivity, stupidity, or at least a deficient ability of abstract thought and logical argument. Sexist definitions of femininity commonly include all these qualities. In addition, the female has a special emotional capacity for sympathy and compassion. The most striking point of difference regards sexual propensies – while the female is under-sexed the African is over-sexed.

Both racist and sexist conceptions variously emphasise the dependence of the black and the woman. Both include a set of beliefs about the inferiority of the group in question, its incapacity to perform certain roles and to exercise authority because of certain innate qualities, and various ideas about the desirability of social distance. Both racism and sexism are deterministic belief systems. Incapacities and inequalities are attributed to innate genetic differences. Both have a dual ascriptive basis – in biological science and in theology. In the case of sexism this involves both arguments drawn from biology – women's 'maternal instinct', 'lesser physical strength' and so on – as well as justifications from theological texts. Both racist and sexist ideologies are ubiquitous in South African society and are elaborated and inculcated in such institutions as the churches, educational institutions, media and primarily the family – the site of both the primary socialisation of children and the stabilisation of adult personalities. They could also be said to locate the subordinate group outside the 'mainstream' – blacks in the Bantustans and women in the home.

It is the convergence of the systems of racial and sexual domination that creates the particular edge of oppression experienced by black women. While all women earn less than men, it is black women's wages which are the lowest; while far fewer women than men reach tertiary levels of education, it is black women who make up the smallest group; while all women are denied access to contraception and abortion on demand as part of their right to control their own bodies, it is black women who have the narrowest choices. The latter is clear in terms of the far fewer numbers of black women who have access to legal abortions; in the widespread use of the controversial contraceptive injection, depo-provera, and sterilisation without full consent within some South African hospitals; in the instances where black women are forced to use family-planning devices in order to gain or maintain employment. While all women in South Africa are subject to sexual violence, particularly rape, it is black working-class women who are the most vulnerable. While all women are subject to legal disabilities, those of black women are most intense. Simons (1968) has demonstrated how the colonial rulers interpreted the African indigenous laws in a distorted way which amplified the disadvantages of women. Under present-day customary law all married African women and all women below the age of 21 are defined as legal 'minors'. The male marital power was abolished by the Matrimonial Property Act that came into force in 1984, but this excludes almost all African marriages. Those black women, married by a marriage officer without an antenuptial contract, are automatically married out of community of property, but the husband retains the marital power. This means that the husband acquires guardianship of the wife and she is considered a minor who cannot enter into any binding contract, even a hire purchase agreement, or credit account, without the prior permission of her husband. With the splintering of black family life under the strains of the migrant labour system, many rural women are heads of their households and their material conditions contrast grossly with their subordinate legal status.

It is the convergence of these two systems of racial and sexual domination that creates the particular powerlessness and vulnerability of black women. This frames the 'ultra-exploitability' of domestic workers.

2 Conditions of Service

I have been a slave all my life
Domestic servant, January, 1979

One of the first things I noticed when I landed was
that I was immediately dependent on the services of
men and women who are not of my own colour. I
felt I was in a slave state, and that, too, the very
worst sort of slave state. I mean the sort in which
the slaves are not owned by masters responsible for
their welfare, nor protected by stringent laws from
ill-treatment, but one in which they are nominally
like white people, and can be thrown into the streets
to starve, without pensions, or public relief when
nobody happens to need their services, or when they
are old and are displaced by the young.[1]
*George Bernard Shaw, April 1932, in a message to
South Africa broadcast from Cape Town on the eve
of his departure from the country*

Domestic service is widespread in South Africa. All
the white households in my sample employed domestic workers on
either a full-time or a part-time basis. Many of these workers perceive
themselves as slaves. They are, in fact, a desperately insecure group of
workers, who lack fundamental workers' rights and work for long
hours at extremely low wages for employers who are often indifferent
to their welfare. Their exploitation, in the words of John Rex, is
sometimes 'suggestive of slavery'. (Rex, 1970: 54.)

One domestic worker, the mother of two young children, earns
£9.30 a month and works an 80-hour week.[2] The only time she sees her
children is during her 'off' on Sunday afternoons. The time she goes off
varies because she must serve and wash up her employer's Sunday

lunch. Sometimes, when there are guests, she gets off as late as 3.30 p.m., but usually it is earlier. She sleeps in because her employer, a widow, is too nervous to sleep alone. Even on Sundays she must return to her workplace to sleep.

She is 38 years old and has worked for the same employer for eight years. She has not had a holiday during that period. She is given the occasional day off 'to attend a funeral'. She dreads the holiday season because then her employer's married daughter and her three small children come to stay, which means a good deal of extra work.

She is devoted to her husband, and is extremely anxious that her marriage seems to be breaking up. Her husband is not allowed to sleep over with her, but he used to do so occasionally. He is now involved with a young nurse.

She says the worst thing about her job is not having time to be with her husband and children, and that her employer is constantly joking about how fat she is. She has no hobbies or interests and spends her evenings alone in her room making grass mats which she sells. She cannot belong to any voluntary associations and says she does not see other people much. Her social life consists of conversations with other servants in the nighbourhood on the afternoons when her employer is out playing bridge.

She finds no satisfaction in her work, but feels a good deal of compassion for her employer, who is elderly and has poor sight. She feels trapped in her present job by this sense of pity, and by the lack of any alternatives. She expects, though, that she will have to go on working until her children are educated. It is a source of considerable distress to her that her children see so little of her. She fears 'they do not think of me as their mother'. Her employer is the widow of a retired professional man and is actively involved in community work.

Another domestic worker, aged 42, has been a servant all her working life, having started at the age of 12 as a nanny. She earns £8.30 a month and works a 66-hour week. She has no day off and has had one week's holiday in the four years she has worked for her present employer. She spends about two hours each day walking to and from work. At home, she spends most of her time doing her own domestic work. She has three children. Her husband is a contract worker in Port Elizabeth and comes home for one month each year.

She says the worst thing about her job is that she has 'to live on the smell of meat'. She is given bread, tea, jam and mealie meal, and occasionally manages to steal a piece of meat out of the cooking pot when making stew for her employer's family. She jokes that she much prefers cooking stew to steak or chops, for this reason.

She describes her employer as 'a chameleon, she changes from day to day'. But overall, 'I don't think she has any feelings for me. She looks down on me and shouts at me in front of her children.' Her employer, married to a successful professional man in Grahamstown, describes her as 'one of the family'. Elsie sees herself as 'a slave in the house' and talks a good deal about the difficulty of having to look after two families. Her hopes for the future centre on her children.

These two domestic workers were encountered in a random sample in the Eastern Cape. There is no reason to suppose that they are atypical.

The Domestic Workers

All the domestic workers in the sample of 225 households were female. The majority, 58 per cent, were Xhosa; 40 per cent were Mfengu; and 2 per cent were 'coloured'. The majority were middle-aged women.[3] (In the short questionnaire sample of 125 domestic workers, age was not asked for, but the sample included one 15-year-old girl earning £1.30 a month for a working week of fifty-nine hours.)

This age distribution contrasts strongly with the pattern in pre-industrial Europe. Laslett has shown that:

> Western servants (between 1574 and 1821) were to a very large
> extent young, unmarried persons – indeed, sexually mature
> persons waiting to be married . . . Service in England and the
> West was a stage in the life cycle for large numbers of people.
> (Laslett, 1977: 34.)

Laslett describes these as 'life-cycle servants'. By contrast in contemporary South Africa domestic workers are 'life-long servants'.

The great majority of domestic workers in the Eastern Cape study had only a minimum amount of formal education. 63 per cent had been to school but the vast majority, three-quarters, had not progressed beyond Standard V. No one in the sample had progressed higher than Standard VIII. Only 6 per cent of the depth worker sample, as compared with 64 per cent of the employers, had any other education or were going to classes of any kind. One was going to Red Cross classes, and the other two were attending night school.

Many of the domestic workers in the Eastern Cape sample expressed a deep sense of hopelessness and despondency about their own lives.

Their hopes for the future focused on their children, and education was seen as the means whereby their children could escape to a better life. Education was stressed as 'something nobody can take away from you', and was sometimes considered a kind of insurance policy for their own future:

> I would like to educate my children so when they are finished they can give me money. If they work as domestics they will not be able to give me money and see to themselves.

For these reasons many domestic workers invest a considerable portion of their income in the education of their children. With their low wages, this involves a considerable amount of self-sacrifice.

Given their own extremely deprived educational backgrounds, their educational aspirations for their children were pitched very high. In 90 per cent of the answers in the depth sample there was a sex difference in the occupations they would choose for their cleverest sons and cleverest daughters. All wanted their children to become white-collar workers. The four occupations chosen for the cleverest daughter were nurse (28); teacher (16); social worker (3); and dressmaker (1). The occupations chosen for the cleverest sons covered a wider and more prestigious range. They were teacher (18); doctor (12); farmer (10); lawyer (5); radio announcer (1); clerk (1); minister of religion (1).

Many stressed the importance of education for their daughters so they could avoid having to be domestic workers. None wanted their own children to become domestic servants. Reasons given included:

The low status of the occupation –

We get no respect.

You are not counted as a woman.

Educated people look down on us domestics.

A domestic is not counted as an important person.

Lack of appreciation by employers –

Your employer looks down on you. You have to keep on saying, 'Remember that I am a woman too.'

Our employers look down on us, but our job is important because we do a lot for them.

It lowers your dignity to be a domestic. Your employer's child can swear at you and you have got to laugh. There is nothing you can do. The parents say nothing.

Low wages –

You work very hard and earn very little.

It's hard work, very little money and makes you tired.

Specially on the farm we work hard for nothing.

Long hours –

You have no time to see your friends.

We have to leave our children early in the morning and look after our madam's children. We have no time to look after them even when they are sick.

Lack of pension rights or job securty –

You work for years and get nothing at the end. Not even thank you.

You can be dismissed at any time.

No matter if I work here for one hundred years I can be dismissed for breaking a cup and get nothing. Not even a thank you. I will be classified as stupid. They will forget the years I worked and worry about the cup.

You can't complain or you might lose your job. If you complain your employer tells you about all the girls coming to the door looking for work.

The monotonous and tiring nature of the work –

It's hard work.

It makes you tired and you do the same things every day.

As a domestic you have to do everything. You wash walls, clean windows, clean, tidy, cook and look after the children. I think the employers are just scared of saying go and do gardening as well. You do all that for little money.

> I even have to look after the dogs and cats. The employers think about them more than they think about me. It's not an interesting job. You don't learn from it. It just makes you tired to think you are going to do same thing every day. That is why I have all my children at school.

> Your learn nothing useful, you get bossed around too much. I have to be at work before sunrise in winter. It's hard.

The attitudes towards their jobs expressed in these statements underline the pathos of the situation in which many domestic workers are trapped. The irony is that they are driven into domestic employment in order to support their dependants, and then have to neglect their own families in the process. Many domestic workers are also migrant workers who have left their families and friends behind them. As in nineteenth-century Britain, domestic service is a route of access to urban-industrial society. It is an occupational role that allows for movement into an urban setting, a different class context, and at least the possibility of social mobility.

The most common route to survival for men in the Eastern Cape involves migration to the mines; the most common route for women involves migration to domestic service. In studies of migrant labour this aspect is frequently neglected. Certainly the distance covered is far shorter for women. All the domestic workers in the depth sample had been born in the Eastern Cape; 26 per cent on farms and 10 per cent in Grahamstown. Seventy-two per cent had lived in their present location for between 15 and 20 years. Seventeen per cent of the total worker sample lived in the rural areas of the Eastern Cape. Farm people often come into Grahamstown unofficially and illegally. As unregistered domestic workers they are in an especially vulnerable position. Regular inspections by the Department of Bantu Administration and Development involve a considerable risk of being caught as an unregistered domestic worker.[4] Mayer found that:

> There is a competitive advantage in willingness to accept lower wages and longer hours; a combined effect of what people were used to on the farm and their illegal situation in town. Town women complain openly that farm women spoil the local domestic labour market. 'They will work from morning till night for R20 a month.' (Mayer, 1979: 75.)

While many women come into Grahamstown as migrant domestic workers, many women also leave the area. In Grahamstown about a quarter of the 2800 work contracts currently registered for other cities are for women, mostly for domestic jobs in Port Elizabeth and Uitenhage.[5] Willsworth reports negative responses from domestic workers returning from jobs in Port Elizabeth. Things there were 'different', 'too fast', 'the madam didn't understand me', 'the madam talked too fast', 'the madam was cold'. Most of them said they preferred being 'home', even though women in domestic employment in their home areas made many of the same comments about their employers. (Willsworth, 1979: 115.) Relationships with employers are a crucial part of the domestic worker's situation. As perceived by the workers, these relationships are not generally as warm, close and supportive as many whites apparently believe them to be.

Wages

Masters, give unto your servants that which is just and equal; knowing that ye also have a master in heaven. (Colossians 4:1.)

This was quoted to me by a Baptist minister who pays his servant £16 a month. He expressed considerable concern about the wages paid to domestic servants in the Eastern Cape. In his view 'a just wage' is an essential starting point for people who are trying to organise their lives around Christian principles. Although the majority of the employers I interviewed claimed to be Christians and to belong to a church, few paid their domestic servants a living, let alone a just wage.

In my sample of 225 households, wages ranged from £1.20 (in two cases) to £20 (in one case) a month. Of the 175 domestic worker informants, 157 were full-time workers as defined by a working week of at least forty hours. They earned an average of £7.60 per month. The average calculated from the employers' answers was somewhat higher. The employer sample included thirty-six full-time workers. Of the thirty-five answers given by employers (one refused to answer the question), the average was £8.20 a month.

In one case, the worker had started at £1 a month and was now earning £10 a month, after seventeen years' service.

There was no guarantee that the wage would be increased regularly each year. Most received irregular increases in their wage, and not one worker knew how much it would be increased by during the next year. As one worker expressed it, 'She gives me an increase when she feels like it.' Several said that they were too afraid of losing their jobs to ask for an increase.

> I tried complaining that I cannot afford my children's school fees, but she said she is also struggling. I am afraid she will sack me if I speak again.

Others said they had given up trying to ask for increased wages.

> I always wait until she gives me an increase. Once when I tried to ask for an increase she told me in a low voice that I must never ask for an increase. I must just wait, because her husband never asked for an increase when he was employed by other people. He worked hard until he got himself his own job. Now he has a garage of his own.

> I, was told I must never ask for an increase because her husband does not ask for an increase at Fort England.

In the Eastern Cape there seems to be no bargaining over wages when the domestic worker is initially employed. This reflects their atomised, vulnerable position as workers. In 74 per cent of the depth sample the worker was told by her employer what she would be paid. In the remaining 26 per cent the servant started work without knowing how much she would be paid; she simply waited until the end of the month to see what her first payment would be. Overall, wages appear to be settled entirely by the employer, in a haphazard way decidedly disadvantageous to the worker.

In fact the domestic worker is in much the same position as Elsie, the domestic servant in Arnold Bennett's novel, *Riceyman Steps.* Her employer, Mr Earlforward, is about to marry Mrs Arb, who opens the conversation:

> 'Now, I expect Mr Earlforward's settled your wages with you.'
> 'No, 'm.'
> 'Not said anything at all?'
> 'No, 'm. But it'll be all right.'
> 'Now what wages do you want, Elsie?'
> 'I prefer to leave it to you, 'm.'
> 'Well of course, Elsie, being a "general" is a very different thing from being a char. You have a good home and all your food. And a regular situation . . .'
> Her wage was settled at 20 pounds a year.

Of course, conditions in South Africa today can only be compared with those in Britain a century ago, when the country was divided by extreme class inequalities and the working classes lacked political power as well as educational and unemployment opportunities.

It is significant that Stewart's *Xhosa Phrase Book and Vocabulary*, first printed in 1899 and reprinted in 1906 and 1976, contains a section entitled 'About work in the House' in which wage negotiation proceeds as follows:

What wages do you want?
I want sixteen shillings a month.

or:

I want a pound a month.
That is too much; I cannot give that, till I see how you work.
What will you give me?
I will give you fourteen shillings a month and your food.
I agree to that.

Clearly the manner in which the starting wage is arrived at reflects the vulnerability and powerlessness of the worker *vis-à-vis* her employer. Whisson and Weil point out that this fixing of wages by the employer without consultation with the worker is 'the "traditional relationship" in South Africa. The employer states the terms and the employee accepts them without attempting to negotiate.' (Whisson and Weil, 1971: 3.) The domestic worker can hardly do so, as she is trapped within a structure of constraints which leave her little choice of alternative employment or life-style.

Two arguments are frequently heard to justify the payment of such low cash wages: one to do with the unskilled nature of the work involved; and the other with payment 'in kind'. Both these arguments present difficulties. In the first case it must be stressed that domestic labour is not a simple commodity. While it is traditionally regarded as an unskilled occupation, in fact there is an enormous range in the demands made upon the worker, the skills expected, the knowledge assumed, and the trust and responsibility involved. While one employer may expect her worker to do only the simplest of cleaning work another may require of her extremely complicated and personal services.

The majority of the domestic workers in the Eastern Cape depth sample, 84 per cent, did general domestic work. Only 6 per cent did no cooking. The workers interviewed demonstrated an extremely wide range of skills. Some seemed to be doing all the household work plus a range of jobs from cleaning the car, to doing the shopping, to bathing, brushing and walking the employer's dogs. A number of the employers, 20 per cent, said they did no domestic work themselves, and of those who said that they did the amount was sometimes extremely limited. For example, one employer who said she did domestic work could only list 'tidying of drawers' when asked to specify her tasks. In one case where the worker did all the household work, this included shopping and ordering food over the telephone. For what should be considered the job of a housekeeper she was paid £6 a month.

The duties of domestic workers depend primarily on the size and wealth of the households in which they work, and on the number of workers employed. In small households many roles have to be combined. In the Eastern Cape study the average size of the employer's household was 3.9 persons; 47 lived in houses and three in flats. A small proportion included young children: two households had three children under 6 years of age, and four had two children under 6 years of age. The houses varied from extremely luxurious to small suburban. There were no slum dwellings in the sample.

One of the two largest houses employed two servants to look after its ten rooms; the other had only one. The one-servant household seems to be the norm, at least in the urban areas of the Eastern Cape, and most are 'maids of all work', often overburdened with a combination of drudgery and isolation.[6]

The drudgery is sometimes alleviated by modern household appliances. Most of the servants had access to hot water in the kitchen, and several households contained appliances such as polishers and vacuum cleaners. However, domestic servants are not always allowed to use these and this is often a source of grievance.

> She does have a vacuum cleaner, but I am not allowed to use it. She said I will break it. I must kneel. She uses it when she is at home, then that day is a day of hell.

Another domestic worker who was not allowed to use the vacuum cleaner reported:

> She uses it when she wants to be a devil on me. I use a brush which does not clean as well as the machine. As soon as she

takes that vacuum she says I do not clean properly. I don't know what she pays me for.

In the Eastern Cape, and throughout South Africa generally, payments in kind are frequently used to legitimise low cash wages. Income 'in kind' cannot easily be calculated. For example, payments in kind generally include food supplied, either full board for those living in, or meals at work for those living out. But as Whisson and Weil point out, it is debatable whether this food should 'be valued in terms of what it cost the employer, in terms of the value that it represents to the employer (for example, left-overs that might have been thrown away had the servant not eaten them) . . .' or in terms of what the servant would have spent on the food of her choice. (Whisson and Weil, 1971: 19.)

Writing of domestic service in nineteenth-century Britain, Burnett focuses on the difficulty of estimating the real, as opposed to the money earnings of domestic servants:

> One of the major attractions of the occupation was that it normally offered board and lodging and, for men servants, livery when required, so that the wage was clear of out goings and available for spending, saving or other uses. (Burnett, 1977: 158.)

Burnett implies that in the case of a live-in servant the cash wage is simply 'pocket money'. However, in the total Eastern Cape sample of 225, only 16 per cent of the servants 'lived in'. Hence the 'pocket money' thesis is not generally applicable. Nevertheless it is a widely used rationalisation for the payment of low cash wages. For this reason Macmillan has termed it 'the most pernicious pocket money theory'. He writes:

> I must insist on this as at the root of the most general type of poverty in the world, the poor and solitary woman, and I must insist I am blaming no individual, only a system based on lack of understanding. (Macmillan, 1915: 13.)

In the Eastern Cape, payments in kind vary considerably. All the workers in the depth sample received some food daily. The following items were most frequently mentioned: samp, beans, mealie meal, bread, jam and tea.

In the majority cases, 86 per cent, the food was rationed. Sometimes this rationing is done in minute detail. For example, one employer said she gave her domestic worker:

> One carrot, one tomato or onion, half a pound of samp, two inches of milk, two slices of bread, one piece of 'servants' meat', two tea bags and one spoonful of jam

each day. This employer itemised the above proudly, and reckons that her worker is 'the best fed in Port Alfred'.[7]

A large proportion, 40 per cent, were not allowed to take any food home. However, a total of 82 per cent said they did sometimes take food home for their families, though one said:

> No, there is nothing I could take home. My children know that they must not expect anything from me when I come home from work.

A number of workers, 18 per cent, received the same food as their employers, but the majority, 80 per cent, received 'servants' rations' and one received both.

The 'rationing' of food is subject to different cultural meanings. In traditional Xhosa society everyone is allotted their pre-ordained portions of food according to age, sex and family position. However, in the workplace the practice and language of rationing often conveys hurtful messages of inferiority and reinforces the domestic worker's dependence on her employer.

The quantity and quality of food given varied widely. Almost half, 48 per cent of the depth sample, received no meat at all. This was a particular source of frustration to servants who had to cook meat for their employers two and even three times a day. As one expressed it, 'The smell of meat must be enough for me.' Almost a quarter of the depth sample received meat every day, two twice a week and one once a week.[7] A number of the depth sample said they were allowed to make coffee or tea at any time, but often the quantities were rationed. One domestic servant was given one tea bag every two days; in another case a worker was dismissed for stealing a tea bag.

Just less than a quarter thought they got enough food, and only eight were satisfied with both the quantity and the quality of the food they got. Twenty-four were dissatisfied because they did not get what they considered sufficient meat; ten because they got no fruit or vegetables, and eight because generally the quantities given were considered too small. Some comments were:

I only get samp, but I cook everything and am not allowed to eat it. Everybody would like a piece of meat, specially if you have to cook it. The smell is enough.[8]

I only get samp, bread and jam. I could get TB quite easily.

The smell of their food makes me hungry.

Making pudding for them is the worst. I have to just lick the dish and that's the end.

The only meat I get is what I steal from the pot while the stew is cooking.[8]

Another had to take her food home uncooked. She commented:

I only eat the smell of food because they cook their own meals.

Several were given leftovers from the employer's table. One said:

I'm just a rubbish tin for them.

Clearly, most employers in the Eastern Cape do not share the opinion of Arnold Bennett's Maggie Clayhanger that 'to give inferior food to a servant was . . . the most unforgivable in parsimony'.

Nevertheless, leftovers and hand-me-downs to the domestic worker often mean that she is able to feed and clothe her own children better. Neil Williams has described how a domestic worker:

was allowed to take the food in the pot after her masters had eaten. So we ate well. The faceless, voiceless people she served faithfully gave her some old baby clothes for me to wear. I was always warm. (Williams, 1978: 23.)

Unlike the English domestic worker whose 'greatest horror was the knowledge that I would now have to submit to the badge of servitude – a cap and apron', uniforms are highly prized. Many (62 per cent) of the depth Eastern Cape sample said they were provided with a uniform by their employers, though sometimes this was only an apron. It is not uncommon for this to constitute the domestic servant's Christmas present.

She buys me overalls at Christmas and tells me that it is my Christmas present and I must wear it to work. To avoid trouble I take it as a Christmas present and wear it at work but you shouldn't have to wear your Christmas present to work.

Another worker reacted differently to the same situation.

She gives me overalls and tells me that's my Christmas present and I must wear it to work. But I say a Christmas present is something different. I will never wear it at work. I only wear it when I feel like it to save my clothes. I mean she cannot tell me what to do about it.

Another, when asked what she received last Christmas, replied, 'Only an overall' and did not elaborate further.

Some domestic workers are given old clothing by their employers, though 46 per cent of the depth sample said they received no clothing other than a uniform from their employers for either themselves or members of their families. In a few cases the employers sold their old clothing to their workers.

I buy their old clothes from this little bit of money they give me.

Most domestic workers are given something extra at Christmas. The majority of the domestic servants in the depth sample said they got extra money. The amount given ranged from £1 (in two cases) to £6.60 (one case). Eighty-two per cent of the domestic workers said they received Christmas presents for themselves or their children. These presents maily took the form of groceries and clothing (either old or new). One was given overalls for herself and a pair of socks for her son. Another was given '£1 and a petticoat'; another 'a dish towel, a face cloth and some soap'; another a tiny quantity of meat 'and two cups'. Sometimes workers were given sweets for their children, and in a few cases fairly substantial amounts of groceries such as 'sugar, samp, rice, biscuits, jam and a box of Surf'.

Other forms of cash payment are rare. Only 12 per cent said they were paid overtime for work done outside of their normal hours. Eleven said they were paid extra if there were guests staying in the house, and fifteen said the guests sometimes tipped them. Other times the guests 'just say goodbye'. In only one case was the employer paying into a savings account on her worker's behalf. In no case did the worker know whether her employer would provide a pension for her when she was too old to work.

In a few cases employers help with their workers' children's school fees. In the forty-eight cases in the depth sample where domestic workers had children attending school, only eight said that their employers regularly helped them with their children's schooling expenses. One commented:

> No, she does not care. She does not like our children to go to school because she says they end up nowhere.

Another said, 'She is not interested in that because she says our children don't go far in school.'

Domestic workers usually have access to a service equivalent to medical insurance. This is a beneficial aspect of the paternalistic nature of the relationship between workers and employers within the institution of domestic service. As Roberts found in her study of farm labour in the Eastern Cape:

> the paternalistic nature of the relationship between farmers and their labour usually implies the tacit acceptance by the farmers of an obligation to care for the health of their farm servant.
> (Roberts, 1959: 46.)

Many employers of domestic workers accept the same obligation, though the degree to which this is fulfilled varies extremely widely. The large majority of workers, 98 per cent, were given medicines when they were ill, usually inexpensive aspirin and cough mixture.

A few workers were provided with other facilities such as the use of the employer's stove to cook for themselves, the use of the employer's facilities to wash their own clothes, or the use of a radio. Several said they were not allowed to use the radio or the telephone. Sometimes they had been told this was because they might break them. However 98 per cent said they sometimes used some of these facilities surreptitiously without their employers' knowledge. The one who didn't said it was because her employer 'is always around'. The question 'Do you use any of these facilities without your employer knowing?' elicited some surprising responses. For example, one domestic worker replied, 'Yes, especially the kitchen to eat in.' It transpired that both the domestic workers employed in this household had to eat their meals 'outside, next to the toilet', when the employers were at home, as they usually were.

Another answered:

Yes, especially the radio, but I have to lock the front door so I can hear her when she comes.

One worker was only allowed to use the radio from 9 to 9.30 a.m. for the church service, but did so surreptitiously at other times.

Of course, by acting in this way, domestic workers are conforming to their employers' expectations. Employers expect their workers to cheat and steal, and in doing so the worker accepts and reinforces the master's image of herself. As Genovese has pointed out, writing of slavery in the American south, this also reinforces their inferiority.[9] However, in the vast majority of cases, stealing appears to be a strategy of survival.

This is especially true of farm workers. Their payments in kind generally involve free housing, fuel, water, part rations and the use of a garden plot.[10] One domestic worker earns £2 a month as a domestic servant in a farmer's kitchen. Her husband earns £3 a month as a farm hand. The only food they are given is a tin of mealies once a week for the whole family of six people. They have a small vegetable garden, but half the vegetables they grow have to be given to the 'Madam', to be used in her own kitchen. One farm worker said:

The time has come for us to see that being a domestic is just a waste of time. Although we don't pay rent or buy wood we have to buy clothes, coffee and all the other things, and pay for our children's school fees.

This comment reveals the extent to which payment in kind ignores the fact that most domestic workers have dependants. All the domestic workers interviewed had others besides themselves dependent on their earnings: there was an average of 5.53 dependants per domestic worker.

This finding is confirmed by studies of domestic servants in other areas of South Africa. Preston-Whyte found that 60 per cent of the domestic workers in her Durban study were supporting minor children, and Whisson and Weil quote a survey conducted in Johannesburg in 1970 which estimated that 'on an average each maid has four dependants, namely mother, two children of school-going age and one child of pre-school age. On an average 76 per cent of the minimum expenses for food, clothing and schooling are paid by the maid.' In Cape Town, Whisson and Weil found that 80 per cent of the domestic servants had dependent families. (Preston-Whyte, 1973: 261; Whisson and Weil, 1971: 29.)

Obviously wage calculations in the Eastern Cape do not take account on these responsibilities. Domestic workers on farms are especially exploited. The average wage paid to twenty-eight full-time domestic servants in the rural areas of the Eastern Cape (farms plus the small village of Bathurst) was £4 per month.[11] The low wages paid to domestic workers in the Eastern Cape are confirmed by other sources. According to one, domestic workers in Riebeeck East, a small village 40 kilometres north-west of Grahamstown, earn 'an average fulltime wage of [£3.30] a month.' One woman who 'had worked for the same employer for 30 years earned [£2.60] a month'.[12] The Mayor of Port Alfred has stated, 'The domestic wage paid to those lucky enough to get a job is probably less than [£3.30] a month.'[13] In Grahamstown the situation is not much better.

Domestic workers are not protected by legislation stipulating the minimum wage, hours of work, or other conditions of service. Add to this legal vacuum the lack of disability and unemployment insurance, pensions and paid sick leave, and domestic workers are clearly an extremely insecure group of workers, open to exploitation by their employers. Such exploitation is evident, not only in their low wages, but also in the long hours they work.[14]

Hours

Domestic workers work far longer hours than other workers, with the exception of farm labourers. Most workers in South Africa work between forty and forty-five hours a week and expect at least two weeks' paid holiday annually. In the Eastern Cape study the average is a 61-hour working week for full-time domestic workers.

Such long working hours have also been reported of domestic workers in other areas.[15] In the Eastern Cape study the longest hours were usually worked by live-in servants. The longest hours worked were by three domestic servants who worked eighty-five hours a week, and seven who worked eighty-four. All were live-in servants. This is supported by Whisson and Weil's finding that the average live-in domestic servant in Goodwood worked over sixty hours a week. The longest hours worked in their study were by two young country girls in Goodwood, who put in eighty-four and seventy-eight hours a week, for which the latter received £3. 30 a month. (Whisson and Weil, 1971: 12.)

A living-in domestic worker in the Eastern Cape is frequently considered generally available in the evenings to cook, wash up, baby-sit, serve snacks when her employers return from an evening out or, as in one case, serve coffee at 11 p.m. to their bridge guests. In the latter case the domestic worker started work at 6 a.m. and earned £6 per month, with one Sunday afternoon off per month. Work until late hours is also reported by Meer in her Durban study. (Meer, 1975: 42.) Horn reports cases of servants working from 6 a.m. until midnight in nineteenth-century Britain, but in South Africa today this appears to be the exception rather than the rule.[16] Only in six cases in the depth sample of fifty domestic workers was the worker paid overtime for work done outside her normal hours. As one answered, when asked what was the worst thing about domestic work, 'You never knock off.'

The vast majority started work early in the morning, mostly between 6 and 8 a.m. There was a far greater range in the time at which they usually stopped work for the day. Several mentioned that they had to stay longer if their employer had guests. One who generally went off at 6 p.m. had to stay until between 9 and 10 p.m when her employer entertained.

The majority of workers had between half an hour and an hour off during the day, but several stressed that their time off was extremely rushed.

Like the factory worker who does a 44-hour week, the domestic worker may have to spend a considerable time each day travelling to and from work. This was true of the forty-two living-out workers in the depth sample: twenty-four spent about an hour travelling to and from work; seven spent about half an hour; seven spent about two hours; one spent three hours and three spent a few minutes. Only twelve usually travelled to work by bus. These were all Grahamstown workers; in the other small town in the area of investigation, Port Alfred, no bus service is provided. Thus the majority of the domestic servants in the sample (75 per cent) walked to work. Sometimes this involved a considerable distance. The furthest distance covered in the depth sample involved six kilometres from a luxurious beach-front house in Port Alfred to the domestic worker's two-room dwelling in the township. This distance includes a steep hill and took me one and a half hours one way. The woman who walks this distance of twelve kilometres per day does so six days a week and is 52 years old. She earns £9 a month. In one case the domestic worker left her home shortly after 5 a.m. each day, and reached her place of work at 6.30 a.m. In the evening she left at 6 p.m. and reached home about 7.30 p.m.

Clearly black workers generally in South Africa have to spend considerable time travelling to their workplace. However, it is possible that domestic workers, because of the distance between black and white residential areas, have to spend longer.

If the working day of domestic workers generally is long, that of domestic workers in the rural areas is especially so. No less than 99.9 per cent work more than forty-eight hours per week. The average working week is seventy-three hours and thirty-five minutes. This very generous input in terms of hours is by no means reflected in the wages and, among the full-time domestic workers in the rural areas there was even a low negative correlation (P equals – 0.04) between working hours and wages. This means that there is a very slight inverse relationship – that is, the more hours worked the lower the wages. In the urban areas there was a weak positive correlation (P equals plus 0.2)

Almost a third of the total sample of 175 workers work a seven-day week. Having a day off per week is considered a highly-prized advantage in a job. When asked what was the best thing about their job, several workers mentioned that they got one day off, or an afternoon off, per week. One mother of three small children, who are being brought up by their grandmother, is able to visit them only on her one day off each month.

This pattern contrasts with that which emerged from Preston-Whyte's Durban study, where she found that 'all full-time servants expect, and most receive at least one free day, or afternon per week. This may be, but is not necessarily, in addition to the free Sunday afternoons which are traditionally accepted as the servants' right.' In Morningside and Durban North the majority of employees received both. (Preston-Whyte, 1969: 108.) Weinrich, on the other hand, found in the Fort Victoria study that only 9 per cent of servants have a whole day free each week. (Weinrich, 1976: 239.)

In order to appreciate what is involved in such long working hours, it is important to remember that most black women workers are also domestic workers in their own homes. On arriving home, at whatever time, from whatever work, she often has to cook the evening meal, put the children to bed, and sometimes do washing, cleaning and ironing, before she herself lies down for the night. Most domestic servants said they spent their meagre leisure time doing domestic work in their own homes.

Not only do domestic workers work far longer hours than other workers, but they also receive less paid leave. The norm in industry is two or three weeks of paid leave a year, plus public holidays. As in the case of working hours and wages, there is considerable variation in the amount of paid leave given to domestic workers; however, within this variation certain features emerge clearly. The great majority of the domestic workers in this sample (83.4 per cent) have to work on public holidays. Several mentioned that this was one of the worst features of their jobs.

> I have to work on public holidays instead of enjoying myself in the township with my friends.

A considerable number were given no annual holiday. Overall, 34 per cent were given one week's holiday, or less, each year. Of the eight domestic workers in the depth sample who were given no annual holiday, four had worked for between five and ten years with the same employer, and four for between fifteen and twenty years. In one case no leave had been given during the seventeen years the domestic servant was continuously employed by the same person.

In the Eastern Cape it seems fairly common to take a domestic servant to a holiday house on the coast. Here her duties are often even more onerous, owing to primitive cooking facilities, and more time-consuming, with extra visitors and guests in the house. This is often counted as the domestic worker's holiday. (For this reason, the employers' answers to the question whether servants were given a holiday has not been included in the calculation.) Such 'holidays' are not always popular with domestic workers. When asked to identify a single aspect of their job they would choose to change, one domestic worker replied

> They take me to the sea and when we get back they say did you have a good holiday. But it's no holiday for me.

This practice is especially irksome to those domestic workers who have friends and relatives who are migrant workers and come home for a brief period at Christmas.

Studies of domestic workers in other areas of South Africa report a similar variation in the amount of annual leave granted by employers. (Whisson and Weil, 1971: 19.) Paid leave is not invariably the practice in the Eastern Cape. Only 40 per cent of all the domestic workers interviewed in the Eastern Cape study said they were paid during their annual holiday. It is beyond my comprehension how the remaining employers expect their domestic workers to live during this period.

Less than one third of the depth worker sample spent all Christmas Day with their own families. Fifty-eight per cent spent part of it with their own families; 8 per cent spent none and one was a new worker who did not know what arrangements her employer would make over Christmas. This is a frequent source of grievance. As one worker expressed it:

Even on New Year's Day I don't have off. Even if people come to visit me I have to leave them and go off to work.

Such working conditions appear to be even worse than those of farm workers, the other group of ultra-exploitable and ultra-exploited workers in the Eastern Cape. Antrobus found that the majority of farmers give one to two weeks' leave each year, though 18 per cent of the farmers give no leave at all. (Antrobus, 1976: 15.) In her earlier Eastern Cape study, Roberts found forty-two of the seventy-three farmers visited gave their permanent male workers regular annual paid leave, but only eleven gave more than eight days. She stresses the long hours of farm workers.

Almost all farmers work their labour, in theory at any rate, from sunrise to sunset. In practice this means roughly from 5 a.m. to 7 p.m. in summer and from 7 a.m. to 5.30 p.m. in winter. Most of them allow half an hour off for breakfast and an hour at midday for lunch. (Roberts, 1959: 68.)

Such working hours obviously involve a considerable level of deprivation of family life for the workers involved.

Accommodation

The accommodation provided for residential domestic workers is frequently squalid, or bare and cramped, especially in comparison with the standard of furnishings in the employers' living quarters. The way in which residential homes are often built with servants' quarters at the back, frequently with a separate entrance, creates separate social universes for the two groups. The standard accommodation for domestic workers in the two towns in the Eastern Cape study contains a toilet, and sometimes a shower. Some employers furnish their servants' rooms with a bed and mattress, a chair and table; some provide blankets. Only six of the live-in servants in the Eastern Cape depth sample said they liked their rooms; two said they did not. Only three had access to a bathroom, and only one had hot water available for her personal use. One said she had to 'wash in the toilet with water from the kitchen'. When asked, 'If there was one thing you could add to your room what would it be?' some answered:

> Blankets.
>
> A chair.
>
> A table to put my plate when I eat.

Most servants' rooms that I have seen are drab, bare, small and cheerless. They are reminiscent of Elsie's bedroom, as described by Arnold Bennett in *Riceyman Steps*:

> Its furniture comprised one narrow iron bedstead, one small yellow washstand, one small yellow chest of drawers with a small mirror, one windsor chair, and nothing else in the way of furniture unless the books behind the door could be called furniture. No carpet. No apparatus of illumination except a candle.

But such accommodation has to be seen in several cultural contexts. In Elsie's case her bedroom had:

> one grand, exciting quality. It was solely hers. It was the first bedroom she had ever in all her life had entirely to herself. More, in her personal experience, it was the first room that was used as a bedroom and nothing else.
>
> She had had no privacy. She now gazed on every side and what she saw and felt was privacy; a luxurious sensation, exquisite and hardly credible.

To have a room of one's own, regardless of its size, is a great luxury for the vast majority of those in domestic employment, especially in the context of the acute housing shortage in most black and 'coloured' townships and the difficulties of finding even single accommodation.[17] It is also a luxury compared to the squalid and crowded accommodation many migrant workers live in.[18] It affords some protection from the violence and insecurity of the townships, some of which are among the most 'violent communities in the world'. (Wilson and Thompson,

1971, vol.2: 219.) Clearly residential servants experience a degree of comfort and security in their accommodation which many non-residential servants lack. They often have access to facilities such as electricity and hot water which are not provided in most black township houses. A room of one's own often symbolises independence to the young African girl, as it did to Elsie and to Virginia Woolf. This is especially true for those escaping from the restraints of rural life. Mayer reports a young girl saying:

> girls who had been in East London before told me the most interesting things about it, especially the freedom one enjoys there – a room to yourself, and earning money, and buying anything you like. (Mayer, 1961: 241.)

While 'a room of one's own' may be valued, and domestic service may provide a tenuous escape route from rural poverty, it affords domestic workers little satisfaction. 'Trapped' by poverty, labour controls and lack of employment alternatives, they find they have escaped one set of intolerable circumstances for another.

Domestic workers are deprived of family life, of reasonable working hours, of regular paid leave, of time to pursue social and leisure interests of their own choosing, of a negotiated wage, of decent working conditions, of the ability to rent or purchase accommodation in the area of their choice, of respectful treatment, of acknowledgement of the dignity and necessity of their labour, of legal protection, and of any effective bargaining power.

3 Deprivations

My child does not remember that I am her mother. She
doesn't love me too much and this is difficult for me.
Domestic worker (cited in Lawton, 1985: 77)

Many domestic workers consider the occupation in
which they are trapped to be close to slavery. This is, however, a
perception they share with other Africans in other forms of work.
Africans in South Africa generally are one of the most regimented
labour forces in the contemporary world. Unlike other African
workers, though, domestic workers are situated in a legal vacuum
within this coercive structure, lacking any laws to govern their
employment or to protect them against unfair dismissal.

The great majority of the workers in the Eastern Cape sample had
been domestic workers for most of their working lives – between
twenty and thirty-five years. They all stressed that they had had no
alternative. Most had taken their first jobs as young girls of eighteen
and under; some started at the age of eleven and twelve as 'nannies'
looking after small white children. In answer to the question, 'At what
age did you start your first job?' one woman replied, 'I don't know. I've
been a slave for a long time.'

In many cases their first jobs were as nannies in white households,
and in others it was helping relatives who were domestic workers. Most
of these workers had held jobs with between three and six different
employers. Many feel trapped in their present jobs. Eight farm
domestic workers said their particular job was obligatory through
marriage to a worker on the farm.

The boss told me that I must stop working with chicory. They want
me to work inside the house but I was told I must not steal sugar.

This obligatory domestic service appears to be a fairly common practice. In her study of black communities on European farms in the districts of Albany, Adelaide and Bedford, Hunter found that:

> The earnings of a man employed on a farm are usually supplemented by the earnings of his wife or children. In the districts visited, a family is never hired as a whole; each member is hired and paid separately; but it is understood that if a man is hired, his wife and children must work if, and when, they are needed. On one farm two families, in which the men were quite satisfactory, were dismissed because their wives and daughters refused to work in the house. On another there were only two or three hands because the lady of the house could not get on with maids, and when she quarrelled with a maid the whole family had to go. It is usual for the mistress, when she requires a maid, not to wait for applications for the post, but to send for whatever woman or girl on the farm she wishes. (Hunter 1961: 515.)

Twenty years later Roberts found that in the Eastern Cape:

> many farmers emphasise that one of the conditions of employment of the African family is that the dependants of the head of the household shall make themselves available to the farmer whenever they are required. (Roberts, 1959: 25.)

Another twenty years later, working in the same area, I came across several instances in which families were dismissed because their wives either refused to work in the house, or were not regarded as 'satisfactory' workers. In one case this was a bone of contention between a farmer and his wife. She wanted her husband to dismiss a family including two males whom the husband regarded as satisfactory agricultural labourers, because their female relatives refused to work in the house.

Thus domestic workers on farms appear to be trapped by a web of constraints whereby they are often coerced into domestic service. Resistance may mean that the entire family is left without a place to live or the means to do so.

Most of the domestic workers in the depth sample said they chose this particular job because there were no other jobs available. A few said they had tried various 'informal sector' activities such as hawking vegetables, sewing, dressmaking, brewing, liquor dealing, selling pinecones collected from the forest, selling acorns for pig food, but had been unable to make a living.[1] In answer to the question, 'Have you ever done any other kind of work?' one woman replied:

> I never had that chance. My mother died when I was a day old so other people brought me up. They never bothered even to send me to school. So how could I learn any other kind of work?

In both the towns in the Eastern Cape study domestic workers are extremely easy to obtain. Whites frequently complain about the stream of women coming to their doors asking for work. One newcomer to Grahamstown asked an estate agent how she could obtain a domestic servant and was told:

> Oh, here it's easy. We just pick them up off the streets.

The main mode of recruitment in fact appears to be through personal contact. Of the forty-two urban domestic workers in the depth sample, 70 per cent found out about their present job through a connection of kinship or friendship with the previous or present servant in the house. Only seven did so through approaching their employer directly themselves. The majority of domestic servants had worked for the same employer for a considerable period, between five and twenty-five years.

In the depth sample of fifty domestic workers various reasons were given for having left their last job: five said they moved from the area; fourteen left because their employers moved; two because of marriage; seven because they fell pregnant; eighteen of their own choice and four were dismissed by their employers. Their answers to the question, 'Why did you leave your last job?' are revealing:

> I had a baby and nobody to look after it.

> My husband died so I had to leave that farm. Some farmers don't keep widows, especially if the children are too young to work on the farm.

> I had a baby. I could not keep it because I had to sleep in.

> I had a baby. My husband said I can't get home so late because of the baby, but when he came across a better woman he never thought of me. He just went off with Miss Better.

> I got sick. They don't want you to be sick. You must be as strong as iron.

Dismissal is, of course, usually with immediate effect. Many of these women appear to be caught up in a cycle of poverty, with a lack of education and employment opportunities which continues from generation to generation. This vicious circle leads one to suspect that domestic work may involve a degree of ascription in a quasi-caste status. The mother of two out of every three respondents in the depth sample had also been a domestic worker. In eight cases the mother was a farm labourer. Only in eleven cases had the mother ever been to school.

This pattern contrasts with the development of domestic service in Britain during this century. By the 1920s and 1930s, as new employment opportunities opened up to women, domestic service was no longer the 'natural' outlet for women's employment that it had been in Victorian times. This process of dispersal from domestic work into other occupations has occurred among black men in South Africa, but is only slowly beginning to occur among black women. In Cape Town, Whisson and Weil report that domestic servants largely comprised 'the less educated, less capable and less organised sections of the working population'. (Whisson and Weil, 1971: 11.) This is confirmed by Meer's Durban study which found that 'they had been pushed into the occupation because of their poverty-stricken backgrounds and they were trapped in it because of their low educational qualifications'. (Meer, 1975: 38.) This process is amplified in the Eastern Cape where the majority of black women are poor and ill-educated, with heavy family responsibilities. They remain largely trapped within domestic service.

Family Life

All the domestic workers in the depth sample had children. The average household size was 6.7 persons, and in over half the sample the domestic worker was the sole breadwinner and support of her family. The pressure this involves is intense, given that African women have no access to family 'benefits' or 'allowances'.

One domestic servant had eight children under the age of 16 (six of whom are still at school). She is no longer married and earns £9 a month for an 85-hour week. Another domestic worker with six children earns £7 a month for a 51-hour week. Her husband receives a pension of £6 per month. Another domestic with five children is a widow and earns £12 a month for a 65-hour week. Many of these children are still at school, and one worker had eleven children, seven under the age of 16. She is married to a gardener, and earns £17 a month for a 77-hour week.

All the 175 domestic workers in the Eastern Cape study had people dependent on their earnings besides themselves. The number of dependants ranged from eleven to three people, with an average of 5.5 dependants per domestic worker. In 102 out of the 175 cases, no one else in the family was employed. Thus in 58.3 per cent of the sample the domestic servant was the sole support of her family.

In view of their low wages it is surprising how many servants manage to send money to other members of their family. In almost a third of the depth sample the worker sent money to someone living somewhere else. In eleven of these cases the money was sent regularly, and in five occasionally. The amounts varied from £7 sent by a domestic earning £20 a month to her son, a political detainee, to £1.70 a month. In another case, £3.30 was sent regularly to a relative by a woman earning £7 a month; in another case £1.70 was sent regularly out of £5.30 a month. These stark figures represent great self-denial – a denial of self that is subsumed under the workers' definition of family obligations.

Only 14 per cent of the domestic workers in the depth sample had someone employed somewhere else who sent money to them. Only in one case was this money sent regularly. This consisted of £6.60 a month sent by a son working in Port Elizabeth to his mother, a domestic servant earning £4 a month.

These domestic workers are frequently subject to some degree of what is termed, in the bland language of Social Science, 'family disorganisation'. The majority of the depth sample, 78 per cent, had been married. Only 48 per cent were still married, the others having been widowed (two), divorced or deserted. Over a third had had a church marriage, three a civil rites marriage and nineteen a traditional, customary marriage.

The vast majority, 98 per cent, were married to unskilled workers. In seven cases the husband was employed as a labourer; four were farm workers; seven were gardeners; one was a driver; four were pensioners and one was unemployed.

A quarter of the depth sample did not know what their husbands earned.[2] Where this was known the wages ranged from £12.20 to £3. It appears that farm workers do not always know what they will be paid at the end of the month. The husband of one respondent, who managed a farm for the owner who lived in Peddie, was paid his promised wage of £5 a month only if no farm animals died during the month. Otherwise he received only £3.30 a month. At the time of the interview he had received only £3.30 a month, for doing the job of a farm manager for the previous eight months. He commented:

The animals get sick. What can I do . . . I've got no medicines.

In only half the cases in the depth sample was the husband living at home with his children.

These women are clearly victims of the disruption of family life that the system of migrant labour entails. Many men are forced to leave their homes and families in the Eastern Cape to go as contract workers to the mines and industrial centres such as Port Elizabeth and Uitenhage. Of the twenty-four domestic workers in the depth sample who were still married, only sixteen said they saw their husbands daily; two saw them once or twice a week; three once or twice a month; and three once a year when their migrant worker husbands return home for a brief period. Only in nineteen cases was the domestic worker living at home with her husband. Two live-in workers were married and had husbands living in the same town but had to sleep apart from them. In six cases the worker's husband was working in another town. Of the married live-in workers two said their husbands were allowed to sleep in their rooms sometimes; two were not; three said he did sleep over with her occasionally, but one said she was too afraid of losing her job to risk this. Many of these women expressed considerable anxiety over the disruption of their marital relationships this involved.

I have to sleep in and neglect my husband.

While we are at work other women can play with our husbands.

The picture that emerges from the domestic workers' long working hours and family circumstances is that they experience a considerable deprivation of family life. One of the aspects of the domestic worker's situation which Rex found 'suggestive of slavery' was the extreme limitation on his or her own family life. Of course this is not unique to the domestic worker in South Africa. The same deprivation is imposed on the black father by the migrant labour system. But in the case of the domestic worker it is uniquely vicious, given the pivotal nature of the mother role in African culture.

This deprivation of family life involves an important contradiction. In advanced capitalist societies all women are subject to a system of sexual domination, but their experience of it depends on their location in the class structure. A woman's class position may provide her with mechanisms of escape from the structure of constraints generated by this system. For example, the woman of the property-owning class can 'buy' her way out of domestic roles by employing domestic labour. While in all advanced capitalist societies this is the prerogative of a small minority of upper-class women, in South Africa, because of the system of racial domination, most white women can obtain 'outs' in this way, and most do. Frequently this involves divesting themselves of a considerable part of domestic work and responsibilities, including the care of young children. For example, in several instances, the house and young children were left in the care of the domestic worker, while both parents went out to work. In some instances the children appear to spend more time with the domestic worker than with their parents. Thus, cheap, black, domestic labour is the instrument whereby white women escape from some of the constraints of their domestic roles. They do so at considerable cost to black women, especially mothers.

Many domestic workers stressed that they had to look after two families and had to neglect their own families in the process.

We leave our children early in the morning to look after other women's families and still they don't appreciate us.

Several employers gave as their reason for employing a domestic servant the time it gave them to devote to their children's intellectual and emotional development. Clearly this is done at the expense of black children. One Grahamstown man said the employment of domestic workers explained why 'white people's children don't grow up criminals'. It is not from having everything they need but 'having nannies who watch them every minute of the day' and instil discipline.[3]

All these domestic workers are mothers, some with very young and some with school-going children. All hate to leave their children alone during the day or in the care of others, but they are forced to do so either because they have no other source of income, or because their husbands do not earn enough to maintain their families.

Thirty-three of the workers in the depth sample said their children were living with them at home; seventeen were living with their grandparents or another relative. Thirty-five said they saw their children daily; five once or twice a week; six once or twice a month; one once every two months; and two once a year. One young woman, with three children being brought up by their grandparents on a farm, manages to see them only once a month. A significant number said their children were allowed by their employers to visit them at work; six said they were not; and six did not know. Only fifteen reported that their children did visit them at work.

One worker's children were looked after by neighbours; twelve by 'no one'; twenty-five by a relative, usually the grandmother or an older child. Often the person looking after the children is a daughter who is thus kept out of school in order to run the home. This perpetuates 'the cycle of poverty, inadequate child care and incomplete education.' (Whisson and Weil, 1971: 31.) Only in six cases were the children all grown up and six were in a creche. Only five said they had to pay someone to look after their children. Anxiety was expressed not only by the mothers of pre-school children, but also by those mothers whose children are already of school-going age. They worry because they have no check on what these children do between the time they get home from school and the time their mothers get home. They feel anxious about not being able to be at home to supervise their homework.

This deprivation of family life applies to both kinds of domestic worker. For example, there is the case of Evelyn whose job includes caring for the small children of a couple, both of whom are employed. Evelyn herself is a mother with two children, aged 5 and 2. She does not spend much time with them in the morning as she leaves home at 5 a.m. and returns about 6 p.m. The children are cared for by her sister and her family. She gets every alternate Sunday off. Thus her situation is not very different from that of a live-in domestic worker, such as Regina, who is separated from her only child whom she sees once a week. (See also Whisson and Weil, 1971, and Meer, 1975, for similar cases in Cape Town and Durban.)

The uniquely vicious operation of this system in South Africa is illustrated by a letter to the local newspaper telling of a visit from two policemen to a private house.

The reason for their visit . . . was that we were accommodating an additional African, the maid's three-year-old boy, without a licence. The maid explained that her son normally spent the day with friends while she was at work, but for two days while they were away, she had been forced to bring him with her. He had not slept on the premises and would return each night to the location. This was apparently not legally permitted without the boy having a licence to be with his mother. Under these circumstances my maid was duly fined [£3.30]. (*Eastern Province Herald*, 27.5.1977.)

The tension between the domestic workers' roles of mother and wage-earner is aggravated by the fact that blacks are in the worst position as regards the provision of day-care facilities for the pre-school child. The incident described above illustrates the cruel paradox of a situation that drives a black mother to seek employment to support her family, and then neglect her family in the process.

Social Life

The long hours and lack of holidays of domestic workers clearly also involve a considerable level of deprivation of social life. None of the workers in the depth sample in the Eastern Cape study said they saw their friends daily, and only six said they were satisfied with the frequency with which they saw their friends. Almost three-quarters said they saw their friends only at week-ends; fifteen said they saw their friends only once or twice a month. Some commented:

How can you have time to visit when you have two families to look after.

I don't have time for friends and visiting.

I'm too tired.

I seldom see people . . . I don't have time.

All the workers in the depth sample said they were friendly with other servants in the neighbourhood or area. Nine said they saw them daily, often on the way to and from work; one once or twice a week, but most said they did so 'seldom', and five said 'never'. The majority spent their time together talking and 'moaning about our difficulties'. The cost of living and 'our employers' appear to be the favourite topics of conversation. I suspect that Powell's account of domestic workers' conversations is applicable here:

If 'them' upstairs could have heard the conversations the parlourmaids carried down from upstairs, they would have realised that our impassive expressions and respectful demeanours hid scorn and derision.[3] (Powell, 1970: 54.)

Since many domestic servants socialise on the pavement outside their employers' houses or in the backyards, the appropriate division here seems to be 'inside' and 'outside', rather than 'upstairs' and 'downstairs'.

All the live-out domestic workers said they spent their evenings at home. One said:

I get home so late I don't have an evening. I just go to bed.

Weekends were spent visiting friends, going to church, and doing domestic work in their own homes.

Sometimes we have some home-made beer, and just enjoy ourselves.

I am too tired to go anywhere at weekends.

Only 44 per cent had holidays in another place; this compares with 92 per cent of the employers.

Only seven domestic workers read a daily or weekly newspaper. Almost three-quarters listened to the radio every day. Some did not because:

I don't have a radio. My son promised to buy us one long ago.

Only one domestic worker read any magazines and only one said she had any special hobbies or leisure-time interests, these being 'tennis and music'. Many expressed regret that they did not have time for such things:

No, I am an old lady.

No, I have no time. I am always at work.

No, my age is beating me.

No, I have not been to school enough. I don't like to mix myself with educated people.

No, I have too many problems to have time to enjoy myself.

No, because I have no education. I feel too shy to join anything.

No, if you have not been to school, you always feel small.

Membership of voluntary associations is largely confined to church organisations. Of the depth domestic worker sample, thirty-five belonged to church organisations, one to a ballroom dancing club, and one to a choir. The great majority, 98 per cent, belonged to a church. This compares with 94 per cent of the employers. Over a quarter belonged to African independent churches. In her Fort Victoria study Weinrich reports that 12 per cent of domestic servants belong to African independent churches, especially to the Zionist Church. Similarly, Preston-Whyte found that 20 per cent of all domestic servants were Zionists. She attributed the popularity of this church to the community spirit among church members, for a sense of belonging is very lacking in the social environment of domestic servants. (See Weinrich, 1976: 232.)

Despite their need for a community spirit many domestic workers do not always have the leisure time to attend church meetings and services. In the Eastern Cape study 60 per cent said they went to church 'seldom'. Several expressed regret that they did not have the time to go more often. One woman said she would like to go to church every Sunday but was able to go only once a month, as she got only one Sunday off per month. This statistic compares with 22 per cent of the employers who said they went to church 'seldom'. Many employers expressed guilt rather than regret at so doing. Six domestic servants said they generally went to church once a month; ten went two to three times a month; three went four or more times a month.

Religious activity plays a very important part in black urban dwellers' lives generally. Willsworth reports that one of the main grievances of employees whose jobs involve them in weekend duties is that 'we can't go to church'. This was said by young and old. (Willsworth, 1979: 282.) At the time of writing, I am involved in the case of a middle-aged domestic worker who came to the Grahamstown Advice Office (a voluntary organisation which provides information for black people involved in labour, housing, influx control and other problems) and expressed her fear that 'my church say they won't bury me unless I go more often'. She cannot go more often as she is given only one Sunday off per month. Her employer is one of the most respected members of white Grahamstown society and high in the Anglican church hierarchy.

The lack of leisure time that these women's dual role in production and reproduction involves is also true of women doing other kinds of work. In their study of women textile workers, Westmore and Townsend found only one woman who said she had time to sit back and relax with a newspaper during the week. None had creative hobbies. Westmore and Townsend also point out that 'the role of reproducer as a limitation on the role of wage labourer, has a structural as well as an ideological dimension.' (Westmore and Townsend, 1975: 30.) The isolation of unpaid domestic workers is broken down when they enter social production, but the potential for collective organisation and political action is constrained by the fact of their time-consuming labour. Clearly the paid domestic servant is under a dual disability here because of the privatised, atomised nature of her work and the duplication of work her roles in production and reproduction involve.

This deprivation of social life is amplified in the case of live-in workers. Only 16 per cent of the domestic workers in the Eastern Cape sample lived in, a somewhat lower figure than has been reported for other areas.[4] Their situation has several characteristics of Erving Goffman's conceptualisation of the 'total institution' in *Asylums* (Penguin, 1968.)

The central feature of total institutions can be described as a breakdown of the barriers ordinarily separating the individual's sleeping, working and playing life. 'All aspects of life are conducted in the same place and under the same single authority.' This clearly applies to many live-in domestic workers. '. . . All phases of the day's activities are tightly scheduled, with one activity leading at a prearranged time into the next, the whole sequence of activities being imposed from above by a system of explicit formal rulings and a body of officials.' Clearly there is a good deal of variation here, but in some households the domestic worker is subject to an extreme regimentation, and her work is done within a rigid routine: '. . . the various enforced activities are brought together into a single rational plan purportedly designed to fulfil the official aims of the institution,' in this case the maximum ease, comfort and convenience of the employer. 'Inmates [of total institutions] typically live in the institution and have restricted contact with the world outside the walls.' In many households domestic workers are allowed visitors only at certain hours, and sometimes visits from the opposite sex, even if they are husbands, are prohibited. The long working hours of many live-in and live-out workers often cut them off from their own communities.

'Each grouping tends to conceive of the other in terms of narrow, hostile stereotypes, staff often seeing inmates as bitter, secretive and untrustworthy, while inmates often see staff as condescending, high-handed and mean.' With the addition of 'lazy' to the staff's typification of inmates, and 'bad-tempered' to the inmates' typification of staff,

Goffman could be describing many domestic workers and their employers.

'Social mobility between the two strata is grossly restricted; social distance is typically great and often formally prescribed. Even talk across the boundaries may be conducted in a special tone of voice . . .' For example, the madams who address their domestic servants in broken English at a slower pace, in a tone pitched much higher than usual.[5]

The extent of the social distance maintained by employers between themselves and their domestic workers shows a good deal of variation. Preston-Whyte found that in Ridgeheights, a prosperous Durban upper-middle-class suburb, domestic servants were expected to do all the domestic tasks, largely unassisted and unsupervised by their employers who were out for much of the day. They worked within a rigid routine and the relationship between employers and their domestic servants was 'one of formality and distance'. In Central Flats, a relatively low-income and heterogeneous suburb of Durban, the work demanded of servants was of an unskilled nature. It involved the cleaning and polishing of the house and the heavy laundry. The white women in the home cooked, tidied and did a good deal of washing and ironing. Their relationship with their employees was marked by 'familiarity and by warmth, tolerance and understanding on both sides'. Preston-Whyte emphasises the 'common social environment' of employers and employees in Central Flats, and the links between individuals within this environment. 'Ridgeheights employers were, on the other hand, drawn from a different social class and in particular from urban English homes. They based their behaviour within the master/servant relationship upon the idealised conception of the pattern in upper and middle class British households of the early part of the century in which there was often little intimate contact between the woman of the home and her domestic employees.' (Preston-Whyte, 1975: 2–16.) In Goffman's terms, 'all these restrictions of contact presumably help to maintain the antagonistic stereotypes. Two different social and cultural worlds develop, jogging alongside each other with points of official contact but little mutual penetration.' Of course, this social distance is reinforced by language differences in the South African case.

'In some institutions there is a kind of slavery, with the inmate's full time placed at the convenience of staff.' The domestic workers who put in an 84-or 85-hour week certainly illustrate this.

Total institutions also involve a degree of role dispossession. 'The recruit comes into the establishment with a conception of himself made possible by certain stable social arrangements in his home world. Upon entrance, he is immediately stripped of the support . . . of these . . . In many total institutions the privilege of having visitors or of visiting away from the establishment is completely withheld at first, ensuring a deep, initial break from past roles and an appreciation of role dispossession.' Visitors to domestic servants are often rigidly controlled. And frequently the domestic worker is known to her employers by a different, English name, symbolising her break with her own social roles and cultural identity.

Goffman also points to 'the forced deference pattern of total institutions; inmates are often required to punctuate their social interaction with staff by verbal acts of deference, such as saying "sir". Another instance is the necessity to beg, importune, or humbly ask for little things such as a light for a cigarette, a drink of water, or permission to use the telephone.' In the Eastern Cape domestic workers are almost invariably required to address their employers as 'madam' and 'master' in a respectful tone. This often extends to small children in the employer's family. Servants, on the other hand, are generally addressed in terms reserved for children and inferiors. The domestic worker is usually a 'girl' and the gardener a 'boy'. They are referred to by their first names, their African surnames frequently being quite unknown to their employers. They are often made to enter and exit by a side or back door and domestic workers are frequently seen sitting behind their employers in motor cars. Goffman writes, 'corresponding to the indignities of speech and action required of the inmate are the indignities of treatment others accord him. The standard examples here are verbal or gestural profanities' or 'talking about him or his fellow inmates as if he were not present.' Statements by many domestic workers in the Eastern Cape bear witness to this.[6]

Total institutions are also characterised by the standard issue of uniforms and food. The domestic worker's uniform externalises her position in the social order. 'Servants' rations' consist of inferior food and often include stale, rotten or simply 'left-over' food which the employer considers unsuitable for her own family's consumption.

While the concept of the total institution illuminates the extreme regimentation of many domestic workers' situations, it fails to capture the extreme isolation some of these women endure. Consider, for example, the case described by Meer of Nancy, who is left in sole charge of her employer's house from 7 a.m. until 6 p.m. when the couple return home. They attend evening classes after supper and some evenings they go to the cinema. She is then locked in the flat. Occasionally she has a gossip with other domestic workers when she hangs out the laundry in the open space on the roof. Lacking a room of her own, she sleeps on a mattress on the floor of the living room of her employer's two-room flat. (Meer, 1975: 42–3.) This is a special kind of 'incapsulation.'

In his East London study Mayer found that a few Xhosa women remained incapsulated like the men in their own circle of fellow villagers. Mayer, however, points to 'the absence of any incapsulating social circle' such as that which surrounds the average male migrant. (Mayer, 1961: 245.) Clearly the emotional upheaval involved in rural-urban migration is softened somewhat for men by 'homeboy' arrangements reported by Mayer (1961: 90–150) and Wilson and Mafeje (1963). Preston-Whyte points out that 'the typical pattern of homeboy groupings reported from most South African urban centres eases the introduction of the male migrant into the urban area. Men, particularly on their first visit to town, often come to employment and accommodation found for them by the group of men from their local area who are already in town. This arrangement and the continual help of homeboys mitigate what might otherwise be a complex and bewildering experience, particularly for uneducated men with little experience of the urban system. No such associations exist to sponsor and help female migrants. Preston-Whyte found that female domestic workers made up 74 per cent of the total number of economically active African women in Durban, and of these an overwhelming proportion (particularly those in resident domestic employment) were migrants, of rural origin. She describes them as 'country-rooted' because they visited their homes during their short annual leave, sent money home and 85 per cent had at one time left children or taken them to be reared at rural homes. However in their life styles and aspirations many domestic workers showed an urban orientation. Therefore, in Mayer's terms they were 'double-rooted'. (Preston-Whyte, 1973: 259–64.)

Mayer points out that in East London, as in Durban, domestic service was the most frequent form of employment for the uneducated migrant, and that:

> the conditions of domestic service are unfavourable both to
> incapsulation in town and to frequent home-visiting. There is no
> weekending, for Sunday afternoon is the usual extent of the
> servant's free time. A fortnight's leave enables her to go home

once a year . . . At work she lives, usually, in a detached room at
the end of her employer's garden or adjoining the garage. This
situation, while it may enable her to receive visitors fairly freely,
prevents the formation of '*amakhaya*' clusters and the voluntary
restriction of social contacts to people of one's own cultural
background. (Mayer, 1961: 245.)

In Johannesburg it was found that the networks of most domestic
workers were both socially and spatially closed. They tended to
interact with persons similarly employed in the same locality. 'Home
girls' played no particular part in these networks. (Walther, 1968.)
Thus it seems clear that domestic workers experience a particular
deprivation of many normal social contacts. Clearly their residential
arrangements and long working hours leave very little opportunity for
any social or recreational life.

Job Satisfaction

None of the domestic workers in the Eastern Cape depth sample said
they enjoyed domestic work, or derived any sense of fulfilment from it.
Work is a means to an end, rather than an end in itself. The end is
survival in a complex and hostile society which often seems to deny
even this modest goal.

When asked 'What would you say is the worst thing about your job?'
some answered:

The worst thing is you don't knock off. (This worker started
work at 6 a.m. and stopped between 8 and 9 p.m. six and a half
days a week.)

Not eating what I cook.

Cooking the dog's food and not eating it.

Window cleaning and making fudge because then the Madam
moans a lot about her sugar.

Baking cakes and roasting meat and not eating it.

Looking after the dogs and cats.[7]

Working on public holidays and not enjoying yourself with
friends in the township.

I never sleep at home with my husband and children. Even if I have a half day off, I have to come back and sleep here at night. (This worker works a 76-hour week.)

Looking after the pigs and the dogs. (A farm domestic worker.)

Washing cars. I feel so bad when people walk past me and see a woman doing that kind of work.

To be called a 'domestic'.

The children are rude. They don't count us as people. They think we belong to their parents.

It's work even when the employers go away on holiday; you have to look after the house, the dogs and the cats.

It's hard work, with no respect or appreciation from your employers and very little money.

I leave for home after supper about 7.30 p.m. It's late. I only work for one person but she won't let me put her supper in the oven. She said to me she likes her food to come straight out of the pan on to the plate.

Having no time off.

Only having a half day a week off.

I sleep in. They don't have an exact time for supper, so I go off late.

Making the fire first thing in the morning.

Making a fire. Although there is a gas stove, I am not allowed to use it.

The master is a nuisance. He comes into the kitchen and tastes the food and says things, but I can do nothing.

Getting home so late.

Ironing and looking after the children at the same time. My employer expects me to do everything.

Her shouting and telling the master everything.

Not being allowed to sit in the kitchen. We have to eat outside next to the toilet and it smells worse than hell.

Many domestic workers referred to specific tasks in their work routine: window cleaning and looking after the dogs and cats were mentioned most frequently. Several mentioned the monotony and boredom of doing the same tasks every day.

When asked 'What would you say is the best thing about your job?' many domestic workers seemed to have difficulty answering.

There is nothing good to say. My job is hell.

But others said:

She doesn't rush me with my work.

There are no small children.

That I am on my own with the children during the day.

Sometimes they eat out and then I get home a little earlier.

I have two weeks' holiday. Many servants don't have that.

Nothing, but at least I have a job.

Half a loaf is better than no bread.

Perhaps that sometimes her daughter gives me a tip or a jersey but then my employer moans and says she is spoiling me.

I am allowed to sleep at home.

When asked, 'If there was one thing about your job you could change, what would that be?' some answered:

Looking after the dogs.

They should not treat us like slaves.

Cleaning windows. I have to climb a ladder. One day I wanted to throw myself to the ground so she would not tell me to clean windows. But I would have broken a leg and gained nothing.

Getting home so late. (This worker leaves work at 7.30 p.m., having started at 7 a.m.) Sometimes I have a sick child and I don't even have time to look after it.

I would prefer not to sleep in, especially because I am married. My husband can find other women while I am sleeping here.

Looking after the dogs. I even have to wash them once a week.

I would like to get a holiday at Christmas but my employer is old. She has nowhere to go so I can't leave her.

Their work is often monotonous drudgery, carried on for immensely long hours with very little aid from machinery.

All the domestic workers in the Eastern Cape study said they found domestic work boring rather than interesting. All said they found that they had too much to get through during the day. Only 10 per cent of the depth sample said they felt lonely in the job. Several who answered in the negative added, 'Because I have so much to do.'[8] Over a third of the depth worker sample (36 per cent) felt their employer supervised their work too closely and bossed them around too much.

She tells me to do one hundred things a day.

The supervision is killing me.

The supervision is too much . . . I can't stand it. Everybody wants to tell me what to do and how to do it.[9]

The privatised nature of the work, the high degree of observability in work performance as well as the close supervision it often involves, are among the reasons for the unpopularity of domestic work.[10]

Just under half of the depth sample thought they were learning useful skills on the job. Many said they were learning skills such as making sweets, cakes and cold drinks, but these were of no use to them, because they did not have the money to buy the ingredients to make them for their own families.

I can't help anybody with what I have learnt because we don't have what our employers have.

No, because it's things I cannot do at home.

Yes, I have learned how to cook and roast the meat that I cannot eat.

I am not interested in what I am learning because it will not help me or my children.

This contrasts with domestic service in nineteenth-century Britain which, Burnett emphasises, provided the opportunities for both learning useful skills and social mobility.[11]

Lenin described domestic work as 'barbarously unproductive, petty, nerve-wracking, stultifying and crushing drudgery', and it has been suggested that the biggest single 'brain drain' in industrialised societies today is 'down the kitchen sink'. (Gould-Davis, 1973: 333.) These are extreme views. Compared with factory work there are opportunities for creative and satisfying work in a domestic context. Some domestic workers take pride in the cleanliness of the homes, and a pleasure in the care of children left in their charge. Some may prefer the apparently easier routines of domestic work to the hard, driving routine of the factory. But much domestic work is of an uncongenial kind and is extremely monotonous and repetitive. Also it should be stressed that domestic work is often of a physically demanding nature, for example, moving furniture, turning mattresses, carrying heavy loads of laundry, and so on. 'Although the tasks that make up housework are dissimilar, there is said to be a sameness about them, which derives from their frequent need to be repeated, their lack of intrinsic meaning, and the impermanence of the goals they achieve.' (Oakley, 1974: 80.) Speaking generally, it appears that those who glorify domestic work rarely engage in it.[12]

In Oakley's study of a group of London housewives, the predominant feeling was one of dissatisfaction with domestic work. In reply to direct questions, 90 per cent of the housewives in the sample reported 'fragmentation'; 75 per cent 'monotony'; and 50 per cent 'time pressures'. She compared these with Goldthorpe's results on factory workers and concluded that housewives in Britain 'experience more monotony, fragmentation, and speed in their work than do workers in the factory'. (Oakley, 1974: 87.) All the women in her sample reported feeling tied to the house and isolated from meaningful social contacts. Given that domestic work in another's home is even more privatised and may be even more solitary; given that it involves following a work routine that is imposed by the employer's orders, rather than evolved for oneself, it seems that Oakley's findings would be duplicated, with a heightened intensity, if applied to domestic workers in South Africa.

It is also arguable that paid domestic work in other people's homes involves an exposure to a particular set of frustrations and resentments, generated by the extreme asymmetry of power and wealth involved. For example, Pollak argues that domestic service 'exposes many women to the frustration of a daily experience of difference between their own standard of living and the living standards of their employers. Such a situation exists in hardly any other line of work. To see what other people have, and what she herself does not have, can almost be called the essential job experience of the domestic servant.' (Pollak, 1950: 144.) Writing in the USA in the late 1940s, Pollak states that 'in our time of class antagonism and in our country of race antagonism in which domestic workers are frequently coloured or at least members of another ethnic group than their employers, the situation is psychologically mined. Logically it must lead to a tremendous amount of pent-up resentment which cannot help but create a desire for aggressive compensation.' (Pollak, 1950: 160.)

Clearly this applies to the South African situation even more sharply because the cultural gap, social inferiority and economic disparity involved are even greater. Pollak argues that the envy, frustration and resentment this inequality generates often lead to criminal behaviour of a peculiarly 'masked' type. Here Pollak points to three factors concerning domestic thefts: first the comparative insignificance of her thefts, not only in the domestic's own eyes but also in her employer's, makes this offence not sufficiently injurious to warrant much vigour in prosecution; second, the employee-employer relationship often leads to an inclination towards leniency on the part of the latter which makes dismissal rather than criminal prosecution the normal consequence; and third, the domestic worker's opportunity to bide her time in the committing of the offence and cover her tracks successfully. For these reasons he asserts that domestic workers are one of the largest groups of female unprosecuted offenders. (Pollak, 1950: 136–8.)

The masked nature of female crime and the occupational frustrations of females in domestic employment suggested by Pollak echo the insights of Lombroso and Ferrero's 1895 study of *The Female Offender*, published in London by T. Fisher Unwin. They argued that female thieves in Italy included a large proportion of domestic servants and quoted Tarnowsky as saying that '49 per cent of female thieves belong to the class of domestic servants'. They relate this to the temptations domestic work affords: 'Girls come up from the country and enter houses where the great or relative well-being which reigns seems to them a sign of enormous wealth. They are badly paid, yet are given money, plate and other valuables to handle, which awake in them *the greed innate in every woman* [my italics] . . .' In the South African context, domestic theft reinforces the stereotypic conception of blacks as innately dishonest, childlike and unreliable.

Many of these negative aspects of domestic work in terms of experiences and evaluations apply in all advanced capitalist societies. What is at stake is fundamentally a class relationship, which in South

African society assumes a racial form. The class nature of this relationship is illustrated by the similarities between employers' perceptions of domestic servants in eighteenth- and nineteenth-century England, and contemporary race attitudes in South Africa. The class nature of the dominant attitudes in Britain is very clear. As one domestic worker remarked bitterly, 'This locking things up makes people dishonest; it's as though because one is working class one is not to be trusted.' (Horn, 1975: 178) Similarly disparate class experiences are used to reinforce the negative stereotypic attitudes of the dominant class. In England many working-class girls 'were frequently called stupid, because they were unacquainted with the names and uses of kitchen articles, whereas it is simply ignorance from not having seen or used them'. (Horn, 1975: 34.) 'Stupidity' and 'dishonesty' are both class-based components of hegemonic ideologies.

While these negative experiences and typifications of domestic work apply in all advanced capitalist societies, and assume a racial form in the South African class structure, it is also arguable that in South Africa the system of racial domination gives a special 'twist' to these experiences. It could be argued that because of their structural location in the South African social formation, blacks employed as domestic servants experience apartheid in a peculiarly humiliating way. Their duties as workers may force them into situations where as blacks their rights are denied or restricted. In Port Elizabeth, for instance, 'domestic servants looking after white children are allowed on white beaches but are not allowed to swim'. (Statement by the Municipal Director of Parks, reported in the *Eastern Province Herald*, 15.1.1977.) In one case three domestic servants were charged for doing so.

Status

In Southern African society domestic service is the least prestigious of all occupations. To appreciate what is involved here, domestic work must be located in a cultural context, as well as in an economic system. As Davidoff emphasises, the context and meaning of domestic work are culturally defined and culturally variable. We should ask: who does it, where, on what occasions and for what reasons? For example, sweeping a floor is an activity which has technologically changed very little. It may be a form of ritual that involves making patterns with magical or aesthetic meanings; it may also be a form of humiliation and punishment as in the army, prisons and some mental hospitals, where the most menial domestic work is used as discipline to keep order.

Nor is domestic work invariably performed by women. The cross-cultural evidence is that very often such tasks as fuel-gathering, simple cooking and cleaning, child-minding and water-carrying have been allocated to young children, and old and handicapped people of either sex; that is, to people too physically weak or socially marginal to be involved in more valued tasks. In fourteenth- and fifteenth-century England, upper-class boys did domestic service in aristocratic households, and in many parts of colonial Africa it was often the 'native' men who performed domestic work for the dominant group.

In South Africa domestic service is predominantly a black female institution. Certainly there is a Xhosa tradition of women doing domestic work, which is institutionalised in the role of the *umtshakazi*, the period of service of the new wife. *Umtshakazi* involves a severe training for womanhood with the emphasis on obedience and deference. The 'Red' Xhosa wife spends several years in her mother-in-law's homestead doing all the domestic work under her direction.

> A bride when married is taken to the hut of her mother-in-law
> and there she spends a year or more 'cooking' for her mother-in-
> law. She is expected to be very humble and *kutele* [diligent], rising
> before any one else, clearing the ashes, cooking, and generally
> acting as a servant in the household . . . Many brides have to
> work extremely hard and often become thin and old-looking soon
> after marriage. (Hunter, 1933: 264.)

Similarly in Bhaca society, the young bride must work for her mother-in-law. '. . . All the heavy work of the household is relegated to her.' (Hammond-Tooke, 1962: 114.)

The young Xhosa woman is socialised into a domestic role; however, the traditional Xhosa practice does not include domestic work for wages. Ideally a woman, especially a woman with small children, should work (*ukusebenza*) in the home, but she should not work (*ukuphangela*) outside the home for wages. (Mayer, 1979: 74.) Thus for the Red Xhosa, paid domestic employment for a young mother is at variance with the dominant role definitions. For both Red and 'School' Xhosa, domestic work is contrasted unfavourably with so-called clean occupations.[13] In the Eastern Cape study, most respondents, at some stage in the interview, complained about the low standing of domestic workers in terms of prestige.

This is confirmed by other studies of domestic workers. Weinrich found that domestic worker and street cleaner were the two occupations which received the lowest prestige rating. (Weinrich, 1973: 122.) Walther reports that Soweto dwellers often tease domestic workers by saying *unoblind*, 'you have blindness', or *uyisilima*, 'you are a fool', because they are employed in work notorious for its long working hours, little leisure time and poor pay. Domestic workers are also called *inyama yezinja*, 'dog's meat', by workers in other occupational roles, for it is said that employers tend to buy them inexpensive and 'horrid' meat, and/or because they receive insufficient food and meat. Similarly Preston-Whyte found that:

> domestic service is the least prestigious of all occupations open to Africans in Durban and nearly all those women seeking employment in this field do so from urgent necessity alone. (Preston-Whyte, 1973: 260.)

According to one view, domestic work in other people's homes *per se* is demeaning. For example, du Bois writes in his essay. 'The Servant in the House':

> the personal degradation of their [domestic servants'] work is so great, that any white man of decency would rather cut his daughter's throat than let her grow up to such a destiny. (Du Bois, 1920: 116.)

According to another view, domestic work in other people's homes is especially degrading for men:

> It is the considered opinion of African society that domestic service is no proper occupation for a man. It is seen as degrading him in his manhood and of providing him with no promotion possibilities and chances of bettering himself. (Weinrich, 1976: 242.)

Weinrich, writing about Rhodesia (now Zimbabwe), goes on to argue that the situation is different for African women:

> For them . . . domestic work is not degrading as it is for African men because cooking has always been the normal work expected of African women . . . For them, far fewer occupations have opened up than for African men, and for those with less than professional training domestic service is practically the only job opportunity available. (Weinrich, 1976: 242–3.)

She concludes that 'if domestic service is to remain an integral part of the Rhodesian way of life, it would be to the advantage of Africans if servants were predominantly women and not men'. This seems a dangerous kind of circular argument which can only operate to reinforce the many disabilities of African women. This is not, however, to deny the extra dimension of ultra-exploitation of male domestic servants, whose occupational role violates traditional gender role definitions.

Overall, a number of factors – both economic and social – contribute to the low status of domestic service. As Burnett has written of domestic servants in nineteenth-century Britain:

> Material disadvantages were no doubt important – the limited opportunites for promotion, the large degree of mechanical repetition in the work, the length and irregularity of working hours, the lack of free time and the ineffectiveness of labour organisations. Yet it was the social disabilities which ultimately weighed more heavily: the isolation of the servant, both from his employer and from the community outside, the virtual absence of a private life, the degree of control exercised by the employer, the use of the term 'servant'. (Burnett, 1977: 172.)

Yet Burnett also suggests (p. 170) that 'the fundamental reason for the low social status of domestic workers must . . . have been the degrading, and sometimes inhuman conditions under which many of them worked'. In both nineteenth-century Britain and contemporary South Africa it is the extreme vulnerability and powerlessness of domestic workers, their ultra-exploitability, that is at the root of this. It is their extremely weak bargaining position in relation to their employers that enables them to command only very low wages and poor working conditions. Their weak bargaining position reflects their deprivation of critical rights as workers.

Worker Rights

The domestic worker is deprived of critical rights as a worker, especially the 'right' (defined as such in advanced capitalist societies) to collective bargaining and legal protection. Domestic workers are in a legal vacuum. There are no laws stipulating the minimum wages, hours of work or other conditions of service. They are not covered by the provisions of the Industrial Conciliation Act (28 of 1956) nor by the Wages Act (5 of 1957). The latter authorises statutory boards to fix minimum wages, but does not apply to farm and domestic workers, the two largest categories of African women wage-earners. In South Africa's industrial laws the domestic servant is excluded as a worker. Wages, conditions of service such as hours of work, rest periods, paid holidays and other benefits are fixed for other workers in South Africa in terms of the Shops and Offices Act (75 of 1964), and the Factories, Machinery and Building Work Act (22 of 1941). For domestic workers these are drawn up arbitrarily by the employer. Domestic workers are excluded from the benefits of the Unemployment Insurance Fund and the Workmen's Compensation Act.[14] Concomitantly, both domestic and agricultural workers do not qualify for maternity benefits. As domestic workers are often the sole supporters of their families, the loss of earnings during pregnancy is an extreme deprivation.

Even the repeal of the Masters and Servants legislation is a mixed blessing. Under this legislation, desertion by a servant was a criminal offence, as was refusal to obey a lawful order. In the Cape, wages could be held back by an employer to pay off debts the servant owed him, but unless prior agreement had been entered into, deductions for breakages were illegal unless the employer could successfully prove 'dereliction of duty' in court. Deductions for breakages are now sometimes threatened by employers. Loaded as the Masters and Servants Act was against the domestic worker, its repeal has left her no legal protection at all.

The lack of disability and unemployment insurance, pensions, maternity benefits and paid sick leave mean that domestic workers are an extremely insecure group. This insecurity is illustrated by the fact that instant dismissal is frequently resorted to by some employers who often fail to observe the common law provisions relating to the issuing of notice and payment in lieu of notice. The insecurity of domestic workers and their vulnerability to instant dismissal on unreasonable grounds is illustrated by the following case from a Grahamstown Advice Office report.

Mrs D. was employed by a family living in Grahamstown. She had worked for Mrs H. for a period of three years and her salary was [£10] per month. She was dismissed because she was 'hopeless'. Dismissal was with immediate effect. We phoned Mrs H. to ask whether she would consider paying Mrs D. notice money. She said she was not prepared to. She felt she was well within her rights because Mrs D. had broken her 'contract'.

According to Mrs H., Mrs D. was an unsatisfactory 'girl' and she told us the following to substantiate her claim:

Mrs H. had gone out one cold wet afternoon leaving the children in Mrs D.'s care. When she came home she found that Mrs D. had allowed the children to play outside and they had got wet. The children developed colds and a doctor was sent for and he prescribed medication. Mrs H. deducted the doctor's bill from Mrs D.'s salary because she claimed Mrs D. had been negligent and irresponsible in allowing the children to play outside.

In such cases of instant dismissal the Advice Office directors report that:

unfortunately we are unable to push very hard since the employers often assert that the employee was drunk, dishonest, 'cheeky', or in some other way abused the agreement between employer and employee. It is then the white madam's word against the domestic worker's, and we often do not succeed in obtaining the normal considerations surrounding termination of employment. The common law is just not enough. (Grahamstown Advice Office report for 1 June–10 December 1977: K. Satchwell and R. van Wyk Smith.)

This threat of instant dismissal illustrates a further dimension of the domestic worker's vulnerability.

Domestic servants lack critical rights as workers. They lack the right to a negotiated wage and favourable working conditions, membership of an effective workers' organisation, to have their families living with them, to rent or purchase accommodation in a place of their choice, to respectful treatment, to the further acquisition of knowledge and skills, to opportunities and scope for advancement, to sell their labour in the place of their choice, to an acknowledgement of their contribution to society and the dignity of their labour. (Some efforts to improve the situation of domestic workers are being made, and these are described in Chapter 7.)

The difficulties in organising such atomised workers into organisations for collective bargaining are as formidable as the importance of the task. Organising domestic workers into unions, even in less coercive and exploitative societies than South Africa, presented difficulties. Burnett points out that in Britain:

unlike most major occupations in the nineteenth century, domestic service was almost untouched by the growth of trade unions, which might have ameliorated the conditions of employment, improved wages and ultimately raised the status of the occupation. Effective unions would, in any case, have been difficult to organise among workers who were so scattered and widespread, and in this respect domestic servants suffered from the same disadvantages as agricultural labourers. Working normally only with one or two other employees, under the employer's own roof and constant supervision, with no regular free time, and with a work-force predominantly female, the conditions of effective association were all lacking for the domestic servant. Moreover, in an occupation so rigidly authoritarian and hierarchical there was little sense of common purpose or even common injustice . . .[15]

The last point does not apply to domestic workers, at least according to the evidence from the Eastern Cape study. Moreover, reports from the recent strike of Eveready workers in Port Elizabeth hardly suggests that a predominantly female workforce is necessarily a conservative factor.

In Britain between 1891 and 1914 there were three separate attempts to unionise domestic servants, all largely unsuccessful. In 1910 the Domestic Workers Union of Great Britain was formed to demand 'higher wages, two hours free time each day and regular rest days each month'. The scale of the demands is indicative, but its membership had reached only 245 by 1912, and it petered out during World War I when more and more domestic workers took up employment in munitions factories. Clearly because of their vulnerability, exacerbated by their isolated work existence, domestic workers will always be difficult to organise. These difficulties are amplified by the political restraints operating against trade union organisation in South Africa at present.

The domestic worker's low wages, long hours of work which involve considerable levels of deprivation of family and social life, her lack of job satisfaction, low status in the community, and marginal position as a worker, all suggest a situation of ultra-exploitation. While the evidence supporting these seven levels of exploitation has been largely drawn from the Eastern Cape study, it is impossible to 'cordon off' domestic servants in this area from the wider society. Thus evidence has been drawn on from studies of domestic workers in other areas of Southern Africa to support this thesis.

Isolated and impotent, the dissatisfied servant's only weapon is to 'vote with her feet', to withdraw her labour and try to find a more congenial place. This is not always easy.

Domestic service in Britain was an extremely mobile occupation involving a very high labour turnover. Domestic servants frequently moved for promotion or simply a change of scene. Many women servants regarded the occupation as almost casual and migrated easily into various trades, shop work, and, later, factory work. In the Eastern Cape, however, domestic service is not a very mobile occupation for two obvious reasons: first, the labour controls on black movement generally; second, the high levels of unemployment in the Eastern Cape. In Port Alfred, for instance, only 1800 of the town's black population of 9000 have jobs. (*Eastern Province Herald*, 7.11.1978.) In Grahamstown, while population and employment figures are notoriously unreliable, there are said to be 4707 black men and 4920 black women in employment, the women mainly in domestic service. A further 1895 men and 747 women are in employment outside Grahamstown, mainly in the Port Elizabeth-Uitenhage areas. Official figures on unemployment registered 1547 men and 4864 women against a total population of 52,004 blacks in Grahamstown and the surrounding area. (*Eastern Province Herald*, 29.8.1978.)

Given these high levels of unemployment, despite their low wages and long hours, those women in domestic service are in a sense 'the lucky ones'. Poverty and lack of employment alternatives, which propel black women into domestic service, mean that legislation coercing them into domestic service is not necessary. Such legislation is not unknown in other societies. For example in Elizabethan England there was an enactment giving power to the Justices of the Peace and the Mayors:

> to send out to service, at fixed rates of remuneration, any
> unmarried women between the ages of 12 and 40 whom they shall
> think fit . . . If any woman shall refuse to serve it shall be lawful
> for the Justices to commit such women to ward until she shall be
> founden to serve.[16]

In South Africa other forms of coercion operate to propel almost 800,000 black women into an occupation few of them would choose.

4 Relations with Employers

I do not know a more agreeable sight than to see servants part of a family.
Mary Wollstonecraft[1]

SOLANGE: Nobody loves me! Nobody loves us!
CLAIRE: *She* does, *she* loves us. She's kind!
         Madame is kind! Madame adores us!
SOLANGE: She loves us the way she loves her
         armchair. Not even *that* much! Like her
         bidet rather. Like her pink enamel toilet
         seat . . .
Jean Genet, The Maids

The family analogy is a major *leitmotif* in the literature on domestic servants. (See for instance, Katzman, 1978: 161–2, writing about industrialising America.) It is widely believed by whites throughout the Eastern Cape that domestic workers are treated as 'one of the family'. A newspaper report on a talk I gave headlined 'Domestics an exploited group, says lecturer' was printed juxtaposed with a story headed 'Tearful farewell to "nanny" of 41 years.' (*Eastern Province Herald*, 3.8.1978.) The story tells of a 'tearful farewell at the Port Elizabeth railway station' when a white employer waved goodbye to her maid after forty-one years' service. The employer was quoted as saying, 'It was like losing one of the family – a very sad affair.' However, in no case in the Eastern Cape depth sample did the domestic worker consider herself one of the family.

Relations between domestic workers and their employers showed considerable variation. In a few situations 'the mistress and servant are practically strangers meeting on the footing of employer and employed, with nothing between them but work and wages'. (Hill, 1869: 225.) Nevertheless, much of the nature of the work involves an intimate contact with the employer: an exposure to stained underwear and family quarrels. In many cases relations were characterised by formality and rigidity. Servants were treated with extreme reserve, and personal interaction was strictly limited to the work situation. In other cases, relations showed a genuine human feeling on both sides, a mutual trust and caring structured on a daily intimacy. However, relations for the most part were highly personalised and showed a degree of 'paternalism' with a sense of superiority on the employer's part, and an intense sense of dependence on the side of the workers. This paternalism is the dominant aspect of the relationship.

The great majority of the employers investigated in the Eastern Cape sample were English-speaking. In her Durban study Preston-Whyte reports an important difference in the general treatment of servants in English- and Afrikaans-speaking homes:

> On the whole Afrikaans-speaking employers tended to be less formal and rigid and more warmly personal in their relationships with employees than were English-speaking employers. (Preston-Whyte, 1969: 145.)

She suggests that an important factor which contributed towards this was the ability of many Afrikaners in all income groups to speak Zulu. In the Eastern Cape study less than half of the workers interviewed in depth said their employer had some knowledge of their home language, which was Xhosa. The majority communicated with their employers in English; only ten in Afrikaans. Preston-Whyte points to the opinion, common amongst African servants,

> that, taken all in all, it is better to work for Afrikaans-speaking families than for English-speaking households. The former have the reputation of understanding Africans and treating them well. (Preston-Whyte, 1969: 243.)

No evidence of this emerged from the Eastern Cape study, but then the question was not directly asked. As it is a largely English-speaking area, the workers may have limited experience of Afrikaans-speaking employers.

Feelings

Only 14 per cent of the depth sample said they did not get along well with their employer. Almost a quarter said they did not like their employer, though several qualified this by saying

I have to like her to earn a living.

Eighty-six per cent thought they were liked by their employers, though this was also often qualified with comments such as:

Because she can't do without a slave like me.

The remaining 14 per cent either did not know or believed that their employers did not like them.

When asked 'What are your feelings towards your employer?' a considerable range of answers was given:

I have no feelings. I am useful to her, that's all.

I like her but her daughter is a spoilt pudding.

I like her because I'm used to her. (This from a worker who had been with the same employer for twenty years.)

They are rude. They don't like us to enjoy ourselves. One time we had a party. Our madam saw us eating. She said, 'You blacks are eating like dogs.'

I have good feelings towards her because she treats me like a person.

I find it easy to communicate with her.

When she was ill I was really worried about her.

I have no feelings for her because she has none for me.

I don't like her but I have to work for her.

I would be sorry if anything happened to her.

I have to fit myself into her.

I feel sorry for her when her children shout at her.

I feel pity for her and try to comfort her when she is upset.

When asked, 'What do you think her feelings are towards you?' the answers again showed a considerable diversity. Often the feeling of being cared for was rooted in some concrete, practical expression. This convinced the domestic worker of the employer's concern.

She has no feelings for me. I am of use to her, that's all.

She thinks I am not fully grown. She treats me like a baby.

She does not see me as a woman. She looks down on me.

I think she likes me. She once knitted my children some jerseys.

I think she feels for me although it's difficult to be sure. It's not something that you can see and touch.

She doesn't care for me. I remember when my mother died she didn't want to give me 'off' although she knows I am the eldest of the family.

I don't know. But she won't get another woman who works like a slave like I do.

She doesn't care for me. I was involved in a bus accident and she took no notice.

She cares about me. When my husband was in hospital she asked me how he was every day.

I think she likes me because she said I could bring my baby to work until I could find someone to look after it.

She has no feeling for me. She doesn't let me go to bed even when she can see I have a cold and she doesn't even give me any medicines so I could get better.

She feels sorry for me when the master shouts at me.

She knows she can cheat me because I am a farm girl.

She doesn't consider me. She doesn't give me time off to see my children or my friends.

She cares for me. When my husband died she helped with the funeral expenses.

She likes me. When my children come to see me she allows them to sleep here.

I don't know. She does not like me to tell her about my problems.

She doesn't care for me. When my maintenance order goes through (the court) she says she will reduce my wages from [£2.30] to [£2.10] a month.

If she cared about me she would not pay me so little. (R25 a month, about £8.30).

She pretends to like me. She keeps on saying I am part of their family.

She thinks she owns me like she owns her motor car.

The notion of 'ownership' is not restricted to employers. An advertisement in the Grahamstown newspaper under 'Situations Wanted' reads as follows:

A.N., cook/general seeks work as owner transferred. (*Grocott's Daily Mail*, 16.2.1979.)

When asked 'What sort of person do you think your employer is?' the most frequently mentioned qualities were changeability and inscrutability. For instance:

She wears a mask with me.

She changes like a chameleon.

Several employers felt they had to convey an air of competence and authority in order to maintain the proper degree of social distance between themselves and their servants. Sometimes this was done with difficulty. For instance, one employer told the writer that when teaching the servant a new recipe she would memorise it in her bedroom beforehand. If she forgot a step she would pretend she needed a handkerchief and retreat to the bedroom where she could look it up privately. This employer felt strongly that one should not reveal any vulnerability to a servant.

There was a considerable range of answers to the question about the sort of person the servant thought her employer was:

She's a horrible person.

Moody. Sometimes she gets up on the wrong side of the bed.

Horrible.

She is a devil.

She's a good person. She considers me. (This from a married live-in worker who said the worst thing about her job was never being able to sleep at home with her husband and children.)

A nice person – I don't call her madam, I call her aunt.

She's a difficult person, not easy to get along with.

An easy person, she tells me if she does not like what I have done.

She is lazy. She sits a lot on the stoep outside while I have to rush around.

She is not easy to know.

She does not want to talk. She is a really white woman.

A peculiar person.

Hard.

She is a very nice person. I think she knows that she pays me very little (R20 per month, about £6.60) so she tries to cover it up by not bossing me too much.

She does not want me to know her.

She is a horrible person. I am sorry to say that because you have to give this to a white person to read, but that's how she is.

When asked about the qualities domestic workers liked the most about their employers, the answers were revealing:

If she has lost something as soon as she finds it she tells me. She does not let me look for it for ever.

She lends me money.

If I have no food at home she buys me some and takes it off my salary at the end of the month.

She takes me home sometimes because we have no buses here. (Port Alfred.)

If she makes tea she gives me some too.

She gives me a loan when I need it.

She helps me with the housework and we have tea together.

She speaks out if she's not happy with me.

She lends me money but she always wants to know what I am going to do with it.

She swears at me in a polite kind of way.

She helps with her children when she is at home.

When we have a quarrel she doesn't tell the master about it.

She does not keep things inside her. If I upset her she tells me.

She does greet me in the mornings.

Answers to this, and to the following question, 'What do you like the least about your employer?' reveal very clearly the average domestic worker's sense of powerlessness and vulnerability (indignation over the accusation of theft was the most frequent theme):

She forgets a lot. She can give you her dress as a present but after a while she searches all over for it.

She likes to accuse us of stealing if she can't find something. When she finds it she doesn't tell us. It's bad.

She loses things and accuses me of stealing them.

Their children don't respect us. They swear at us and the parents say nothing.

The whole family is rude to us.

She always takes her children's side when they are rude to me.

Sometimes she looks at me in a sour way.

When she goes away I have to look after her dogs.

Nothing, because she hides her feelings when she is angry.

She forgets a lot. When she can't find things she says they are walking out of this house.

I have nothing to moan about.

When she loses her purse she shouts at me. When she finds it she doesn't tell me or apologise.

She tells me to look for her purse. If I don't find it she says her purse has feet. But if she finds it she doesn't tell me.

When we fight about something she threatens that she will tell the master.

She gets up late in the mornings.

She give me 'hot chips' (a scolding) for nothing.

She gives her old clothes to her daughter who gives them to her maid.

She always looks at her watch when I come in the morning.

She treats me like a stupid child.

She checks up on me at night. She rings this bell until I wake up. As soon as I put the light on she shouts that it is all right.

She tells stories to the master about me.

Many of the domestic workers' comments show that they feel that employers perceive them only in their occupational role. This one-dimensional perception is seen to involve a denial of their human feelings and needs. Memmi has suggested that this depersonalisation is characteristic of the colonisers's stereotyped conception of the colonised. (Memmi, 1974: 85.) Such depersonalisation is illustrated by the fact that only 10 per cent of the employers in the depth sample knew their domestic workers' full names. In Victorian England, servants were deliberately depersonalised and often called by standardised names, whatever their real names might be. (Davidoff, 1973: 88.) In the Eastern Cape black women are generally called 'Sissy', which indicates something of the same depersonalisation mechanism at work.[2] In a few instances the domestic servant was called 'Cookie'; however, most employers knew their servants' English first names and addressed them by such.[3]

Most relationships between employers and their domestic servants showed a degree of social distance. In only 24 per cent of the cases in the depth domestic worker sample did the employer discuss her problems with her servant. However, 80 per cent of the domestic workers said they discussed their personal and family problems with their employer. One proud worker was the exception:

She is a woman. If she doesn't tell me her problems how can I tell her mine?

Often these problems relate to legislation affecting blacks and black township life. Frequently the domestic worker is dependent on the expertise and good will of employers in untangling the complex skein of restrictions in which black people's lives are enmeshed. Only twelve of the domestic workers said their employers ever discussed political events or Bantu Area Affairs Board policy with them. Only six said they knew any secrets about their employer's family or family members.

Many workers complained that their employers did not appreciate them. Eighteen per cent said their employers never praised or thanked them for the work they did. One worker whose employer has never praised or thanked her during twenty years of service, and who is presently earning £2.30 a month, commented:

> Sometimes I feel ashamed of myself for wasting all those years when they don't appreciate me.

Over half of the depth sample were extremely appreciative of such praise and gratitude:

> I feel good and want to do more.

> I feel very important especially when she decided that rather than go to hospital I would look after her.

> It makes me happy.

However, two workers said they were indifferent and twelve were cynical:

> I feel good but I also feel angry because I know she just wants me to do more.

> I just laugh.

> I feel she just wants me to work hard for nothing.

> I take it as a joke because I don't know whether she means it or not.

> Sometimes I feel like a fool. It's like giving a sweet to a child.

Overall, the relationship between domestic workers and their employers is coloured by the dramatic difference in living standards between the two groups. In nineteenth-century Britain it was observed that:

> Domestic service is full of anomalies. The servant grows
> accustomed to a style of living which is beyond her means if she
> returns to dwell with her own class. (Hill, 1869: 225.)

In contemporary South Africa the problem is not 'becoming accustomed' to a higher standard of living, but being exposed to one at very close quarters. This generates a powerful sense of deprivation.

In the depth sample, domestic workers were asked 'Is there a great difference between the living standards of yourself and your family and your employer and her family, for example in the kind of clothes you can afford to buy, the kind of house you live in and the kind of food you can afford to eat?' All the domestic workers said there was a great difference. The great majority, 80 per cent, thought this difference was unjust; two said it was a matter of indifference to them; and eight thought it was a question of luck.

None had any idea of their employer's household income. However, 66 per cent thought their employers were 'very rich', and 34 per cent thought they were 'rich'. One said 'very rich' because 'the master has his own garage and the madam is a nurse at the hospital'. This domestic worker was paid £6.60 a month for a 66-hour week.

Several said that very rich people were the worst to work for because 'they are greedy'.

> They don't know how to share.

> Rich ones always want more for themselves.

> Ordinary employers pay better because they know how we
> struggle with a little money.

Many of the domestic servants' 'deficiencies' in their employers' eyes derive from this difference in living standards, and the extremely simple home conditions of most blacks in South Africa. Often the elaborate cooking, eating and household arrangements of their white employers are quite outside their own social experience.

Punishment

When asked 'What does your employer do when you have done

something wrong or badly in your job?' some answers were:

She shouts at me.

She deducts from my pay if I break things. If you work with things they can break but she does not care about that.

She shouts her lungs out.

She shouts at me and says she does not know what kind of person I am.

She says nothing but then one of the children will say, 'My mother is cross because you did that,' so you know that she does talk when you are not around.

She sulks.

She pulls a long face for a few days.

She shouts a lot and says that if she sacks me I will be sent to the Ciskei where there are no jobs.

She just tells me to concentrate on my job and not think about other things.

She talks to me as if I was a stupid child.

She tells her friends over tea. That embarrasses me.

She shouts at me like . . . I don't know what. I won't say like a dog because she likes her dogs and cats.

These answers contrast sharply with the employers' answer to the same question.

While domestic workers are subject to a good deal of psychological violence, physical violence is rare. The literature on domestic servants in pre-industrial Britain contains many accounts of servants being subjected to physical punishments. Sometimes the perpetrators are respected historical figures. For instance, the diary of Samuel Pepys includes an entry for 19 February 1665 which describes how the enraged master forced his wife 'to the disturbance of the house and the neighbours, to beat our little girl and then shut her down in the cellar and there she lay all night'. Several colonial twentieth-century societies made provision for the physical chastisement of domestic servants for cheekiness and other wrongdoing.[4] A number of farm workers told

Roberts that 'twenty or thirty years ago beating was the recognised punishment for all workers on the farms' but that it was at present exceptional.

> It appears that most farmers punish their adult male workers either by remonstrating with them verbally, or by docking small privileges or one or more of the subsidiary rations like tobacco. Many of them punish the youths by beating them but most said this practice is dying out. (Roberts, 1959: 70.)

No instances of physical punishments were recorded in the Eastern Cape sample. I was told of two cases where domestic workers had been severely beaten by their employers in the Eastern Cape, but these could not be verified. I was also told of an employer who put ground glass in the sugar to stop her servant from stealing it. The employer who reported this thought it was rather a joke.

It is difficult to make generalisations about physical cruelty to domestic servants. The main source of difficulty is the hidden, or masked, nature of domestic crime generally. One such case surfaced during the period of fieldwork. A man was found guilty in the Supreme Court (Transvaal Provincial Division) of murdering his 15-year-old housemaid by beating her with a *sjambok*. Among the extenuating circumstances found by the judge in the man's favour were:

> his heavy drinking on the day of the murder *and the fact that he had honestly believed the girl had stolen goods.* [my italics]

His counsel claimed that the couple 'had beaten the girl to get the truth out of her about the goods she had allegedly stolen, and not to kill her'. It was found that the man:

> and his wife assaulted the girl repeatedly with a *sjambok* on April 29th, 1978, after suspecting that she had stolen a camera and hairdryer belonging to Mrs Botha.

The judge rejected Botha's evidence that:

> When he had told one of his employees to bring him barbed wire to tie up the girl, it was just to frighten her.

Botha was jailed for ten years; his wife was found guilty of culpable homicide and jailed for three years. (*Eastern Province Herald*, 16.9.1978.) This sentence provoked a letter of protest to the local newspaper entitled 'Ten Years is not enough'. It ended:

> Botha will be free at the age of 42, and the housemaid will be dust in an early grave, guilty or not guilty. (*Eastern Province Herald*, 5.10.1978.)

The masked nature of intra-familial violence generally suggests that only a small proportion of such cases will surface to be processed in the courts.

Sexual Exploitation

Domestic service in South Africa is largely a black female institution. Monica Wilson points out that 'the historical importance of this has been overlooked'. (Wilson, 1972: 13.) The social implications have also been neglected. First, there is the possibility that female domestic workers are open to sexual exploitation. The literature on domestic service in Victorian Britain contains many instances of this. While no instances of sexual exploitation were encountered in the Eastern Cape depth sample of fifty domestic workers, instances have been reported from other studies. For example, Preston-Whyte found that 'in Stamford Hill there was evidence of sexual relationships between European males, both residents and lodgers, and the female servants'. Although 'no instances were encountered from within the unit studied, at least two cases were reported of African women workers for single men in the nearby blocks of flats of whom sexual favours were demanded along with their normal domestic workload'. (Preston-Whyte, 1969: 140, 143.)

From this perspective, it is arguable that the one piece of legislation which operated to 'protect' domestic workers was the Immorality Act, which prohibited sexual relations between members of different social groups. Andreski has pointed to this 'positive aspect' of the Act. He suggests that under the circumstances of great inequality of power and wealth in the servant/employer relationship, this Act:

> protects the women of the burdened races from sexual exploitation by their masters, of the kind to which domestic servants were exposed even in Puritan England, and which remains commonplace in most poor countries of Latin America. (Andreski, 1971: 28.)

This Act was repealed in 1987, and feminists have warned that this may increase the vulnerability of black women workers generally to sexual harassment.

The second implication of domestic service being a predominantly female institution is that it avoids the particular tensions generated by racist stereotypes where domestic servants are predominantly male. This tension is illustrated in Inglis's account of the White Women's Protection Ordinance passed in Papua in 1926, which similarly prohibited sexual relations between members of different racial groups. One source quoted by Inglis explains the agitation for the legislation as follows:

> There has been a number of cases of assault on white women by native servants and others; some serious, others quite trivial. Public opinion, spurred by feminine resentment, rose to a high pitch. The white women of Port Moresby, many of them quite new to tropical conditions, did not seem to understand that the native servants are human . . . There were many of them inclined to be careless about their dress, and unduly familiar with their native servants – far more careless than they would think of being with men of their own colour, and the natives reacted as might be expected from people barely removed from savagery. (Inglis, 1975: 85.)

This kind of behaviour refers to instances such as a white 'madam' in the shower, finding she had no towel, and calling to the 'houseboy' to bring her one. However, Inglis questions any explanation of this ordinance that rests mainly on the behaviour of the white women, whether on their harsh exclusiveness or on their lax familiarity towards their servants. She accounts for this ordinance in terms of the sexual anxiety generated by racist stereotypes:

> Sexual self doubts might easily worry the minds of husbands and fathers confronted daily by totally unfamiliar black male servants, and these doubts when added to a belief in the greater potency of black men, provided the basis for fear of sexual attack. (Inglis, 1975: 24.)

She shows how this legislation was extremely harsh and discriminatory by the standards of the time. It involved savage sentences until it was repealed in 1958. The death penalty for *attempted* rape was the core of the ordinance.

Dependence

Overall, the relationship between domestic workers and their employers is intensely paternalistic. This has two implications: it consigns the worker to a dependent and powerless position and it generates a sense of power and superiority in the employer.

Clearly, in many white South African families, household maintenance depends largely on the skill and hard work of domestic servants. Yet domestic servants are in no real sense members of the households they serve. They are dependants for whom employers assume differing degrees of responsibility, in various combinations of authority and affection. They are given privileges, but not rights, and have no sense of job security.

Within this framework, with its connotation of employer power and worker dependence, the feelings of workers ranged widely. In the best of relationships the employer is viewed as a source of strength and support, especially in helping the servant untangle herself from the mass of laws and restrictions which bind the lives of black people. In the worst relationships, the employer is viewed as an exploiter whose indifference is characteristic of white people generally. This dependence both reflects and reinforces the structural location of black women in South African society.

Most relationships showed some degree of social distance, and some level of depersonalisation. As the chapter on the employers will show, servants are not expected or required to have thoughts, opinions, feelings or identities beyond those necessary for the discharge of their duties. The 'correct' performance of their duties often involves a degree of obsequiousness. This is a general characteristic of 'greedy institutions', a term coined by Coser (1974) which describes domestic service.

Greedy institutions make total claims on their members, seeking exclusive and undivided loyalty and attempting to 'reduce the claims of competing roles and status positions on those they wish to encompass within their boundaries. Their demands on the person are omnivorous.' As Coser points out, there are overlaps between such greedy institutions and Goffman's notion of total institutions. However, they operate through different mechanisms. Greedy institutions, 'though they may in some cases utilize the device of physical isolation, tend to rely mainly on non-physical mechanisms to separate the insider from the outsider and to erect symbolic boundaries between them . . . Nor are greedy institutions marked by external coercion. On the contrary, they tend to rely on voluntary compliance and to evolve means of activating loyalty and commitment.' (Coser, 1974: 4, 6.)

Payment in kind is an important mechanism by which the employers of domestic servants promote this personal loyalty and commitment from their employees. It has been shown above that payment in kind is often of a fairly haphazard nature. Contributions towards children's schooling expenses, clinic fees, presents of clothing, and extra money, clothing and food at Christmas are given as gifts from the employer to her servant.

The importance of such gift relationships has been recognised in anthropological studies. Mauss has noted how they help to reinforce the social hierarchy by promoting feelings of loyalty, faithfulness and gratitude. He writes:

> to give is to show one's superiority, to show that one is something
> more and higher, that one is *magister*. To accept without
> returning or repaying more is to face subordination, to become a
> client and subservient, to become *minister*. (Mauss, 1970: 72.)

Thus the gifts given by employers to their domestic servants help to cement their loyalty and reinforce the hierarchical nature of the relationship between them. This is not to deny the often sincere generosity of employers. It is simply to focus on the status-enhancing properties of such gifts which operate to secure the loyalty of the servant within an extremely hierarchical, unequal relationship. Such gifts also operate to maintain some kind of equilibrium. As expressions of the employer's generosity and benevolence they effectively contain tensions and disguise the conflict of interests inherent in the relationship. But this kind of paternalistic relationship is entirely demeaning for the dependent servant.

> The recipient of a tiny wage, second-hand clothes, food and
> lodgings, 'holidays with the family', medical care and school fees
> for her children, is most completely demeaned. The manner of
> payment implies that she is unable to organise her life properly in
> almost every direction, whether choosing her clothes or saving for
> her children's schooling. (Whisson and Weil, 1971: 42.)

The implication is that the domestic worker is a perpetually irresponsible child.

Rex comes to this conclusion by a different route. He points out that:

> ... just as the system of plantation slavery was accompanied by a growth of the domestic institutions, so is the South African labour system accompanied by an elaborate development of the institution of domestic service. In South Africa of course, as in any other country, domestic service is one of the least free forms of labour in that the servant is thought of as participating only indirectly in the market ... relying for his income and welfare to some extent at least on the benevolence with which his master administers his private household. (Rex, 1974: 53.)

> The sociological key to the domestic servant's situation is that a good part of his real income is provided in kind. This means that, instead of being able to engage in the essence of modern social order, he participates only indirectly through his master's ... household ... He will receive a token wage, but this wage has to be understood as akin to the pocket money which the master might give his child. The essence of the domestic servant's position indeed is that he is a child. And the essence of the master's position is that he is the *paterfamilias* of a household which includes more than simply kin. (Rex, 1974: 53–4.)

The domestic workers' 'childlike' status within this unequal relationship might be expected to reduce them to a kind of degrading sycophancy. However, the researcher was struck by the forceful personalities of many of the women. Writing of domestic servants in Britain, Clapham suggests that:

> relations [between masters and servants] were not always unequal, and there were possibilities of retaliation. Dickens's servants, with their cockney elasticity, and repartee, knew when the scales were inclining their way. (Quoted in Young, 1934: 32.)

In South Africa the situation of domestic servants has been described with insight by Mphahlele, who stresses the complete absence of real communication between master and servant, 'the non-committal antlike way in which blacks serve whites'; the employer's helplessness against her servant's 'cheerful incompetence'; the servants' determination not to be known by their employers:

> This non-committal attitude of the silent servant is his most effective weapon against the white master who has all the instruments of power on his side. Both of them know this. (Mphahlele, 1962: 140.)

The domestic servants' silence, and mockery of employers, might thus be viewed as muted rituals of rebellion. They are a crucial mode of adaptation, a line of resistance that enables the servant to maintain her personality and integrity intact. Petty pilfering, too, might be seen as an expression of situational rebellion. However, given the average domestic servant's low wages, and the high number of dependants, it seems that, at least in the Eastern Cape sample, this is more a strategy of survival than a private revolt.

The evidence given in the following chapter suggests that the domestic worker's main mode of adaptation is the adoption of a mask of deference as a protective disguise. This is generated by the powerlessness of her situation which blocks any overt expression of dissatisfaction.

5 Self Imagery

There is no class less open to democratic ideas than a
contented servant class.
William Clarke (quoted in Burnett, 1977: 172)

The objective deprivation of the domestic worker,
compared to other sections of the workforce in South Africa in terms
of wages, working hours and conditions, is very clear. Yet she displays
few overt signs of dissatisfaction: her voice of complaint is rarely
heard, she does not go on strike, and does not appear to indulge in
much absenteeism. Consequently, she is often viewed as a deferential
worker. This implies an acceptance of the legitimacy of her own
subordination in the social order. The deferential worker 'does not
identify himself with his superiors or strive to reach their status; he
defers to them socially as well as politically'. Thus Lockwood refers to
the domestic worker as the working class's 'most socially acquiescent
and conservative element'. (Lockwood, 1966: 252.)

The image of the obsequious, deferential domestic servant is
widespread in the Eastern Cape. However, the most significant facet of
her overall situation is her relative powerlessness to obtain better
wages and working conditions, owing to the constraints operating
upon domestic workers specifically, and blacks and women generally,
in South Africa. The key to understanding the domestic worker's
situation is dependence. The difference between deference and dependence is crucial. It implies that while the domestic worker does not
endorse her own social subordination, she recognises her powerlessness in the social formation.[1]

The predominant pattern in the Eastern Cape is 'the maid of all
work' or 'cook-general', whose work situation is characterised by
relative isolation and self-containment. She is an atomised worker. In
the workplace, the disparity in income and life-style between worker
and employer is highly visible. The work situation clearly acts as a

model of the wider society as a whole in the minds of many workers. The inequalities of power, wealth and income that they experience at work at the micro-level are reflections of general inequalities.

Most domestic workers reject the legitimacy of such inequalities. This has three implications: they recognise their dependence in the existing structure; they reject the legitimacy of the distribution of power and control within the existing structure; and they then adopt a mask of deference as a way of coping with their situation.

While the majority of domestic workers in the sample tended to view their relationship with their employer as generally a cooperative and harmonious one, these perceptions mainly concern the daily transaction of worker-employer relationships. They do not extend to an acceptance of the legitimacy of the white employers' power over them. Thus while they have a sharp consciousness of exploitation, they generally remain on good terms with individual employers.

While this pragmatic acceptance of their role seems to be the predominant mode of adaptation, different servants' relationships with their employers move off in two directions from this position: some shade into a purely instrumental set of attitudes. Having no personal feelings for their employers, they barely disguise their instrumentality. Other relationships shade off in the opposite direction, and are expressed in a considerable loyalty towards employers whom they perceive as kind and thoughtful. However, all employers expect some degree of deference from their domestic servants.

The evidence that follows suggests that the deference of the domestic worker is more apparent than real. Deference is a mask which is deliberately cultivated to conform to employer expectations, and shield the worker's real feelings. The widespread image among employers of the domestic servant as the deferential worker par excellence is due to two factors: first, the ease with which it fits into the paternalistic racial stereotype – domestic servants are then easily viewed as one of the family; and, second, the powerlessness of the worker's situation, which blocks any overt expression of dissatisfaction with her subordinate position in society. Thus the deference attributed to the domestic worker rests largely on a fallacious inference made from her largely passive social behaviour.

This passivity and acquiescence in the social order must be understood to result from the domestic worker's dependence on her employer, whose power is considerable. It includes the power to hire and fire the worker, as well as to determine her wages, working hours and conditions, and even her right to be living on the farm or in the prescribed urban area.

Such dependence militates against any overt expression of dissatisfaction other than changing jobs. Even this is not always possible in terms of influx control and high levels of black unemployment. In general, therefore, the domestic worker acknowledges her powerlessness and tries to make the best of her inferior situation, while rejecting the legitimacy of it.

The Worker

Only 32 per cent of the workers interviewed said that they were satisfied with their present jobs. Most stressed the scarcity of jobs and the lack of any alternative. Sixty per cent said they would prefer to stay at home and not work. This contrasts strongly with the pattern that emerged from the employer sample, where 62 per cent would ideally choose to be doing part-time work. Many domestic workers stressed that this was not possible for them:

> What can I do? my daughters are just sitting at home having babies every day. They are like chickens laying eggs.

Most have a sense of being exploited, which hinges on what they consider to be their low wages, and lack of appreciation by their employers. Regardless of their perception of their employers' financial circumstances, all the domestic workers in the depth sample thought they should be paid more. Twenty-two thought they should be getting twice as much as they were; seven, three times as much; ten, four times as much; four, five times as much; and seven said they didn't know but thought they should be paid more. Reasons given include the following:

> I have been working for these people for a long time (nineteen years) but am still earning R22 a month (about £7.30). But I am working for rich people. My master is a teacher at Rhodes, my madam teaches at DSG.

> I have brought their children up.

> I do all the work. I even made the fudge and pineapple juice they sell in that shop.

I do all the work in the house and I also have to feed the pigs and the chickens.

Because I have to do the work of two people.

If you could see my baking you would be surprised. It looks like a hotel.

Because I work every day. I never have a day off to enjoy myself with my family.

Because I do all the housework and cooking, look after the dogs, help with the gardening and even wash the cars.

Because I have been with them a long time.

Because I work hard. I look after the house and even the dogs, cats and chickens. I have to sort the eggs very carefully and check if they are first grade.

Because I do everything.

Many mentioned the high cost of living:

We are really struggling.

Because everything is so expensive. We have to buy on HP because we have no money to pay.

Because everything is so expensive. I can hardly buy myself a pair of panties. I don't talk about shoes. They cost my whole month's pay. (A worker earning £5.30 a month for a 66-hour working week.)

We would like to eat the same food and wear the same clothes as them.

All this suggests that a sense of relative deprivation is high among the poor, ill-educated women who form the vast majority of domestic workers in the Eastern Cape. This sense of relative deprivation might be even higher than among some black industrial workers. Fisher quotes a study carried out in East London in January 1974 which 'confirms the impression that relative deprivation is high among black industrial workers':

Workers interviewed were asked what wage they thought they

should be getting. Most workers named a figure approximately double their current wage. Those on R10 suggested R20; those on R20 suggested R40. (Fisher, 1978: 216.)

The majority of domestic workers in the Eastern Cape study thought they should be paid more than double their present wage.

All the employees in the sample thought that domestic workers as a group were 'badly treated'. When asked what could be done to improve the situation of domestic workers, thirty-eight mentioned improved wages; three an organisation of domestic workers; five suggested better communication, and more respectful treatment from their employers; two mentioned a written contract; one a pension after twenty-five years' service; and five said they did not know. Some consciousness of a community of interest emerged. For example, one worker said, 'We are all singing one song. We need the same help with low wages and bad treatment.' Other comments were:

Our employers should be told how important we are.

We should be counted as people.

If we could have some organisation where we could complain without fear of being dismissed.

Our employers should take us as people not as animals.

Our employers should treat us like people not like slaves.

If we could get together with our employers and talk openly about our problems on the table, without worrying about losing our jobs, that might help.

It would help if our madams could be interested in knowing their servants' circumstances. Many madams don't know how many children their maids have.

Another made the same comment and added:

If they knew these things perhaps they would give us better pay.

The Black Person

Genovese has suggested that 'all forms of class oppression have induced some kind of servility and feelings of inferiority in the oppressed; failure to induce these means failure to survive as a system of oppression'. (Genovese, 1971: 6.) A high percentage of the sample, 46 per cent, thought that blacks are generally inferior to whites in their personal qualities. However, many of their answers show some confusion between personal and positional or structural inferiority. For example:

> The whites are sitting on our heads, so we are inferior.

> Whites have everything under the sun . . . we have to be lower than them because we have no money.

> Whites have all the power. They just tell us what they want to do to us.

> We don't have money. The whites are sitting on our necks.

> Yes, but given time we could improve ourselves.

> We are lower than whites because that is where they put us.

A number thought that because blacks and whites are equal in their personal attributes and capacities, whites deliberately keep them down by not paying them enough:

> We can cope. You can put a black person in the forest and just leave water with him or her. We can manage because there is a lot we can do. But now we are chained without money.

> We are equal but we don't have money so we have to beg.

> If we had money we could be more than them.

> We are more capable than whites. That is why they try by all means to keep us under their feet.

> We are potentially equal but we don't have the opportunities to develop ourselves.

All the domestic workers in the depth sample thought that black people are not treated fairly in South Africa. This contrasts with 44 per cent of the employers. The examples of unfair treatment most frequently cited involved passes and influx control. Others involved the lack of employment opportunities, the cost of education, unjust treatment by whites generally, pensions, prison conditions, the lower standard of living of blacks, low wages, transport facilities, poor housing, lack of dignified treatment, ill treatment by the police, inadequate health services . . . the list covers an extremely wide spectrum:

There are so many laws that chain us.

There are very few whites who consider us. They look down on us. When you go to town with your madam she puts you at the back of her van.

Educated blacks have difficulty finding jobs but you will never see an educated white jobless.

We pay for school books and white children don't.

We suffer from many sicknesses because of poverty.

Low wages. These days people like my husband are paid R7 a month (about £3.30) and some mealie meal. (A farm worker.)

We are slaves in our own country.

We are not allowed to join our men when they go and work under contract.

Look at me. I am still working hard at my age (63). But white old ladies don't have to work hard.

The trains that we travel in are not clean.

We don't have comfortable beds like whites have.

We are starving.

What can we do? We are slaves.

Look at how black people are treated at the hospital. If white people were treated like that there would be a big fuss.

Our old people only get their old age pension every second month, but whites get it every month. It's because South Africa is bad.

There are not enough jobs.

We die in jail like flies.

There is no white woman who would do the work I do for so little money.

We are dying like flies because of poverty.

The whites are standing on our necks with their boots.

If you apply for a pension it will take a year to come. In the mean time you have to live on the Holy Spirit.

You have to get permission to go where you want to go.

We are pushed all over the place.

We live in houses that we don't like.

The jails are full of black people. Because we are starving we have to go and steal. We have to steal to live.

On pension days our old people are packed like bags of mealies queueing for their money.

We earn less just because we are blacks.

One day I visited my husband who is working in Port Elizabeth. I didn't know he was living in single men's quarters. I could not sleep with him. He had to contact a friend so I could have a place to sleep. That would never happen to madam.

Even if whites swear at you, you just have to laugh because you might lose your job.

We are not allowed to join our husbands.

We are not counted in this world.

Such discrimination to which blacks are subject in South Africa was the focus of the Black Consciousness movement founded by Steve Biko. During the period of field work almost the entire leadership of the Black Consciousness movement was detained without trial in Grahamstown prison under Section 10 of the Terrorism Act. Before the banning of the Black People's Convention and the Black Community Programme the previous year, the movement had been very active in the Eastern Cape. Four buses and at least two private carloads of people travelled from Grahamstown to King William's Town to attend Biko's funeral in 1977 and were part of the crowd of 30,000. However, only 44 per cent of the depth sample said they had heard of the Black Consciousness movement. (Eleven of these still thought that blacks were generally inferior to whites in their personal qualities.)

When asked what they thought of the Black Consciousness movement some answered:

I am afraid when my children talk about it. I don't want them in jail.

It's a good thing but we all end up in jail. Our leaders die. They hang themselves with trousers and fall out of windows.

We are scared because we hear that black people will be killed if they don't agree with the government.

Very good, but where do we end? Not just in jail, but we die in jail without any charges being brought.

My children keep on telling me about it but I tell them they must please keep away because I don't want them to die young.

I don't want to talk about that. My heart breaks when I think about it. Where are our leaders? Six feet under the ground.

Good, but some die in jail; others get banning orders.

I am scared of it. I hear there is a boy that fell from the building in Port Elizabeth.

We are forgetting that some whites feel sorry for us. We just tie them with one belt.

It would be a good thing if we could turn this world upside down.

We could take over this country. That is why we are put in jail.

Several women said they did not want to talk about the topic. Here it should be emphasised that research among blacks on political attitudes is extremely difficult in the present climate of fear and police harassment in South Africa. Other studies have been unable to obtain much information on political attitudes. For example, Weinrich found that:

Although domestic servants spoke readily about their religion and education, they were most reluctant to express their political attitudes, and I doubt the reliability of the responses we recorded. Many servants were suspicious of any question dealing with politics and often reported these back to their employers. The fact that the interviewers were Europeans, not Africans . . . greatly contributed to the servants' reluctance to speak. (Weinrich, 1976: 233.)

For this reason I employed a black field worker to interview the domestic workers. This chapter pays tribute to her skill. The answers reveal the remarkable extent of trust and confidence she inspired in the respondents.

The Woman

Only a small proportion, 16 per cent of the sample of domestic workers interviewed in depth, thought that women are generally inferior to men in their personal qualities. This contrasts with 24 per cent of their employers. Many black women seemed to have a sense of personal superiority to men, but a structural inferiority. For example:

> We are the same, the problem is that we are women. Otherwise I have more power than my husband. Once he gets into difficulties at home he gives up. Anything difficult . . . he thinks it's the end of the world.

Many women seemed to attribute this sense of superiority to the fact that they had more difficulties to cope with than men, and were generally better able to cope:

> We are more capable than men. Men can't face problems. They think it's the end of the world.

> We are equal but my husband couldn't manage things without me.

> We are far better than men but we have to respect them so we don't lower their dignity.

> Every woman knows we are stronger than men. I don't know about white women if they think the same.

> We are more than them.

> Men's dignity has gone into a bottle of wine.

> Men have lost their dignity in drink.

> Our girls are stronger than men these days.

We are stronger than men but we have to respect them although they don't deserve that respect.

Men are just rubbish.

Men have lost their dignity in many ways. They don't want to look after their families any more.

We give them respect but they are not entitled to it.

We just have to respect our husbands although they don't deserve it. They don't give us enough money to care for our children.

We are stronger. We stand things that our husbands could never stand.

There are some women in detention.

Men are useless these days, they spend all their money on drink.

Our men cannot cope with the responsibility of being the head of the family.

Their husbands' 'irresponsible' handling of money was a common theme:

My husband got a gratuity when he left the BAAB. He wouldn't tell me how much it was. He thought he was a king. He forgot that money will be finished. Now I am the only one who pays the rent, food, everything.

All the domestic workers thought that women were not treated fairly in South Africa. This contrasts with 28 per cent of their employers. However, many of the instances of discrimination they quoted referred to discrimination against blacks generally and black women specifically. For example:

We have to carry passes.

We have to have a permit to visit our husbands.

We are not allowed to join our husbands.

Others implied a feminist consciousness in that they referred specifically to discrimination against them as women:

We work hard like men, but we are paid less.

We are badly treated. Our husbands are making it worse because they don't help us with their own children.

Our men won't tell us what they earn. (This was a common complaint.)

No white woman would work for R9 a month (about £3) as I do.

A white woman can tell you to move a wardrobe. Because you are black she does not think that you are a woman.

Some men don't want to listen to us women.

We get no maternity benefits.

We don't get accommodation of our own.

We have two families to look after, our employers' and our own. The men just go to work and come home. They do not worry about children and other things.

I don't know what my husband earns. I am the one who tries to educate our children. The father does not care.

Men (and 'coloureds') are paid more than us for the same job.

Look at me. I am just like a man who goes to the mines. I only go home at the end of the year.

Our men treat us badly. Our marriages end like paper fires.

While we are at work our husbands find other women.

Men don't want to pay maintenance for their children.

Black men say a woman is a tail.

I am coping with nine children. My husband does not pay a cent.

Our men beat us when they are drunk.

They can take other girl friends even if they are married. We can't do that.

We have to manage our children. You seldom see a man trying to cope alone with his children.

We cope with more. I am coping with my mother and four children on R25 a month (about £8.30). This husband of mine does nothing to help.

Under a quarter had ever heard of the Women's Liberation Movement. This contrasts with 86 per cent of their employers. Interestingly, all of these domestic workers, as opposed to only 6 per cent of their employers, thought it was a good thing. However, several stressed that their daily lives were consumed by other problems:

It's a good thing but I don't have time to liberate myself.

It's good but I worry about my children. What are they going to eat tomorrow?

Compared to their white, mainly middle-class employers these women have a much greater 'feminist consciousness' or insight into discriminations against women. This is clearly related to their location in the social structure. The widespread disruption of family life that the system of migrant labour entails has resulted in the burden of family responsibilities being placed upon black women. Their sense of grievance against what they see as black men's irresponsibility, particularly their drinking habits and secrecy about their incomes, came through very strongly in many interviews. But their indignation about discrimination against women is clearly overshadowed by their consciousness of discrimination against blacks.

The South African

When the domestic workers were asked what they felt about the difference in living standards between themselves and their employers 90 per cent expressed anger or indignation and 10 per cent sadness. All felt strongly about the difference in living standards between black and white South Africans generally.

We are slaves.

The whites are greedy. They only think of their own stomachs.

They live a life of luxury.

South Africa should be ashamed of itself for the way they treat non-whites.

I feel angry when I look at his sheep and goats and we are not allowed to keep any. (A farm worker. None in the rural sample were allowed cattle, sheep, goats or any grazing animals. A few were allowed to keep pigs and chickens.)

It makes me angry especially when I have to serve her tea in bed and she is younger than I am. (A 65-year-old domestic worker.)

Sad – our people are suffering like anything.

Angry – but I'm sure that there are some other whites, like your madam, who also feel strongly about the difference.

It makes me angry to look at their gardens and the food they buy for their dogs. It is better than they buy for us. And the dogs eat off their dishes but we don't.

The whole government is very bad.

South Africa needs to be taken over by the English people and go back to pennies not cents. In those days we were not struggling as much.

I wish the madams would take their maids home and see the kind of houses we are living in.

I hear that in England it's not so bad. Whites work for other whites.

It makes me angry. That is why our children just want to destroy and burn things. They are tired of seeing us suffer.

It makes my heart break. They say things are so expensive but we shop at the same shop. The money she gives me is not even as much as her pocket money.

If God could change it all and turn all the blacks into whites and all the whites into blacks, most of the whites would shoot themselves. They couldn't live with our difficulties.

I don't think our employers must give us all they have, or even half, they must just consider us.

It makes me angry. We are also God's people.

I feel sorry for the whites who care for blacks. We tie them with one rope because we don't know them.

It makes me angry. On rainy days you will stand at the bus stop getting wet and when you get to work your employer tells you how late you are.

It makes me angry. I wish Idi Amin was nearer.

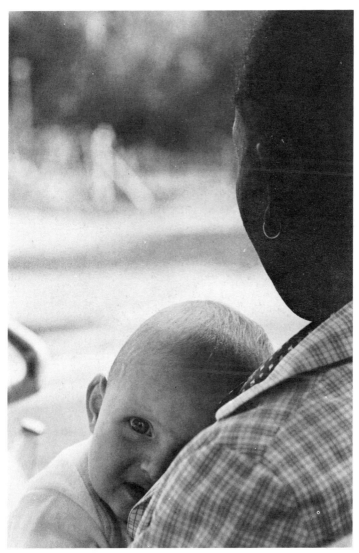

Berea, Johannesburg 1986.
Paul Weinberg/Afrapix

'I start work at 6.30 a.m. I make tea, wake the kids, help them get dressed, make sandwiches for school. When everyone has gone, I put the washing in the machine and clean the house.' Johannesburg, 1986. *Paul Weinberg/Afrapix*

Naumi Seroke (36) is a divorced mother of three. She was too scared to tell her employer that she was pregnant because she felt her employer had enough problems of her own. Her employer was very disappointed in this lack of communication. Baby Neo now lives with her mother and accompanies her while she does the housework. When she is older she will go back to the family home to be looked after by her grandmother. Rustenburg, 1987. *Gisèle Wulfsohn/Afrapix*

'After I've done the main housework, I must walk to the school and fetch the children. Then I iron and see they do their homework, otherwise when the mother comes home she shouts at me and them. Then I must prepare vegetables, bath the kids, fetch pyjamas. When they have supper, I go off to my room.' Johannesburg, 1986. *Paul Weinberg/Afrapix*

'Every December I accompany the family I work for on their annual holiday by the sea. They think that being away from the city is a holiday for me, but I still have to cook, iron, wash and look after the kids.' Plettenberg Bay, Cape Province, 1986. *Gisèle Wulfsohn/Afrapix*

Sarah Molathlegi (32) has worked for a white family in Johannesburg for 7 years. She gets to see her own family in Saulspoort, Bophuthatswana, a few times a year, usually over Christmas or long weekends. Sometimes her son, Titus (11) comes to stay with her in the 'big city'. Saulspoort, 1986. *Gisèle Wulfsohn/Afrapix*

Mrs Mngoma's husband is also a migrant worker in Johannesburg and he lives in a single-sex hostel in the city. She lives in a room on the roof of the block of flats where she is employed. They meet in the city on weekends.
Gisèle Wulfsohn/Afrapix

Sibogile Mngoma (49) is a domestic worker employed by a young white couple in Johannesburg's northern suburbs. She works a 10-hour day and her chores include bed-making, washing, ironing, cleaning and cooking. Johannesburg, 1986. *Gisèle Wulfsohn/Afrapix*

'I want to go to school. I am learning to read and write. Zulu first, then
English. Some people do typing. I would like to learn to type and maybe get
an office job.' Centre of Concern, Sandton, Johannesburg, 1986.
Gisèle Wulfsohn/Afrapix

National launch of SADWU (South African Domestic Workers Union)
Cape Town, November 1986. *Dave Hartman/Afrapix*

Florrie de Villiers (centre), newly elected general secretary of SADWU (South African Domestic Workers Union), Cape Town, November 1986
Dave Hartman/Afrapix

This is unmistakably the language of disaffection; a far cry from T.S Eliot's conception of 'the damp souls of housemaids'.

Expectations of Change

All the domestic servants interviewed in depth, but only 68 per cent of their employers, expect the difference in living standards between blacks and whites to change, though to many domestic workers this change will come about only at some remote time in the future. Almost half of the black respondents thought that though change would come it was impossible to predict when; 28 per cent thought change would come about in their children's lifetime; 10 per cent thought it would come about in their grandchildren's lifetime; and 14 per cent in their own lifetime.

It might take a long time, but whether you like it or not, it is going to change. It might change by means of war but it has to change.

It will change despite Vorster [then Prime Minister]. He is a rubbish.

It will change but it will take time. It is not easy to take a piece of meat out of your mouth and share it.

It will not be easy for whites to give up.

I wish we could fight it out.

It will not change easily. There's going to be a war.

I hope it changes in my lifetime. I would like to see the whites suffer the way we do.

It will take time because even if whites decide to change we will still want to fight them because of the things they have done to us.

It might change in my lifetime, but by then I will be too old to enjoy it.

When asked, 'How do you think you would feel if you had to change places with your employer?' most answers expressed a mixture of incredulity and delight at the prospect.

I would feel good to have a farm of my own and my own slaves.

Oh, I know that will never happen but if it did I would feel proud and I would not like to give her her house back.

I would like to have slaves to look after my dogs and cats.

I would feel very important. All my problems would be little ones which could be solved.

I would feel very happy. My mother would be comfortable and I wouldn't have to worry about leaving her to go to work.

I would feel very good. My children would have their own room.

Very good. I would have a car and my employer would have to walk every day.

I would not like to change places, because I do not want to be like whites.

I would enjoy employing my madam for [£7.10] a month and sitting in my study while she looks after my black child and does the ironing at the same time.

The whole world would be mine.

I would smile all day.

Many workers envisaged this change to mean that they would lead 'a life of luxury'.

When asked whether the domestic worker would behave differently from her employer in any way, answers often combined feelings of revenge with compassion.

I don't see why I should behave differently. I have to do the same to her.

I would behave the same to start with and change later because I couldn't treat another person like she treats me.

I would behave the same. When she is sick I will tell her that my house is not a hospital. That is what she said to me when I was sick.

I would behave the same to start with and loosen the strap later.

I would behave differently. I would be ashamed to treat people like slaves.

I would also give her soup with no meat, beans or vegetables.

What for? I would also ignore the doctor's certificate.

I would give her a lecture.

I would behave the same because she has no heart for me.

I would behave the same and let her suffer like I have done for fifteen years.

I would behave the same way. Later I would change after giving her a lesson.

Yes, I would show her that people must not be treated like animals.

I would behave even worse than she does because some white people think they are made out of white paper and we are made out of steel.

I would not do what she does to me to anybody.

The trouble is that when people have everything they forget about Jesus Christ, our Lord.

I would also make her eat in the toilet when it rains.

I would be even worse and see how long she could take it for.

I would be even tougher than she is.

The resentment expressed in many of these comments suggests an important difference between domestic servants in contemporary South Africa, and in nineteenth-century Britain, in which many servants seem to have been contented with the status quo. Social inequalities were largely unquestioned, especially among the upper servants in large households, many of whom appear to have identified with their employers and bathed in a kind of reflected glory.

In their autobiographical accounts such servants rarely voice resentment or discontent; on the contrary, they stress the responsibilities of their positions, their satisfactions from work well done and the enjoyment to be derived from the community of the servants' hall. In the conflict between social aristocracy and political democracy they were unquestionably on the side of the former. 'There is no class less open to democratic ideas than a contented servant class,' wrote William Clarke. 'Compared with them, their titled and wealthy employers are revolutionists. They cannot bear change, their minds are saturated with the idea of social grades and distinctions, they will not even live with one another on terms of social equality.' (Burnett, 1977: 172.)

While servants in nineteenth-century Britain may have been deferential workers who accepted the legitimacy of their own subordination in the social order, this is clearly not true of domestic workers in contemporary South Africa. In Britain:

the relationship between master and servant depended upon the acceptance of a social 'apartheid', sanctioned by the law of God, and on an economic system which justified sweated labour on the argument of providing work for those otherwise unemployable. When other, more satisfying forms of work became available to women, when religious beliefs waned and when the 'natural' obedience of one class to another came to be widely disputed, this kind of relationship no longer carried with it public approval or private acceptance. (Burnett, 1977: 174.)

In South Africa the relationship between master and servant depends largely on a racial apartheid. Within this pattern the oppression of blacks assumes a more coercive, direct and visible form than class inequalities ever did in Britain. Among servants themselves there is a far more widespread rejection of their subordination in the social order. Unlike nineteenth-century Britain, the deference of domestic workers is a mask, a protective disguise, rather than a psychological reality.

Overall, the multiplicity of images that domestic servants have of themselves as workers, as blacks, as women, and of social relations generally in South Africa, suggests that it is an over-simplification to regard domestic workers as representing a uniform group. However, it would also be incorrect to infer that no generalisations are possible, or that domestic workers do not share certain characteristics of self imagery which can be related to their location in the social structure.[2] It would also be cowardly and evasive not to ask questions about the political implications of such imagery.

Fisher has analysed Mann's notion of 'revolutionary class consciousness' as involving a number of different dimensions:

1 We may say that the individual is objectively deprived, but to what extent does he or she perceive this deprivation? This is the problem of relative deprivation on the individual level.
2 To what extent does the individual who feels deprived perceive a community of interests with other individuals?
3 To what extent does the individual understand the situation in structural terms?
4 To what extent does the individual perceive him/herself or the group as having the power to change the situation?
5 To what extent is an alternative society conceived or conceivable? (Fisher, 1978: 199.)

Fisher writes, 'The first four dimensions involve answers to the following questions: To what extent am I exploited? With whom am I exploited?...[and] by what mechanisms am I exploited? (Fisher, 1978: 199.) To generalise from the self imagery of the domestic workers interviewed in depth, they would appear to answer these questions as follows: I am grossly exploited; I am exploited with other domestic workers specifically, and with blacks generally; I am exploited by the structures of white dominance. Fisher quotes Leggett who uses the term 'class-race' consciousness 'to refer to those who see themselves as belonging to an economically exploited group (a class) which they nevertheless define in racial terms'. (Fisher, 1978: 209.) Giddens has referred to this in suggesting his theory that under certain conditions ethnic characteristics offer a strong source of 'class structuration', the formation of a self-conscious class. (Giddens, 1974: 111–12.)

The evidence from this study suggests that domestic workers possess such a 'class-race consciousness'. Their consciousness appears to involve a high level of relative deprivation as domestic workers, a perception of community of interests with other domestic workers specifically – 'We are all singing one song' – and with blacks generally; and an understanding of the situation in structural terms – 'It will change but it will take time. It is not easy to take a piece of meat out of your mouth and share it.' This understanding involves a deep-seated recognition of powerlessness, and thus little conception of an alternative society, so that a high level of perception of relative deprivation is combined with a sense of impotence. Fisher's elaboration of Sartre's analysis of the process of formation of a 'fused' group out of a 'series' suggests that this present inaction could be suddenly changed.

Earlier I referred to Coser's view of domestic service as 'a greedy institution'. Greedy institutions 'tend to rely on voluntary compliance and to evolve means of activating loyalty and commitment. (Coser, 1974: 4.) Essentially the greedy institution promotes deference relationships which reinforce the legitimacy of the employer's authority. Both the isolation of the domestic worker and the personal and particularistic nature of her relationship with her employer operate to limit access to alternative definitions of the situation. However, the domestic worker is incorporated in domestic service 'from above', not 'from below'. Her real life, rooted in the family obligations which propel her into domestic service in the first place, is outside it. The evidence suggests that this degree of distance gives the domestic worker access to alternative definitions of the situation; definitions which involve a denial of the legitimacy of her subordination within the existing social order.

The image most frequently used by domestic workers to describe their situation was that of slaves, *amakhoboka*:

We are slaves.

We are slaves in our own country.

Our employers should treat us like people and not like slaves.

Rex has pointed to three aspects of the domestic servant's situation in colonial contexts which are 'suggestive of slavery':

There is a tendency to tie him to his job with a specific employer through the introduction of penal sanctions against the servant who breaks his contract; there is an extreme limitation on his or her own family life, since very often he or she is required to live in single quarters; and . . . there is a considerable similarity very often between the way in which a master talks of his servant or is permitted to punish his servant, and what occurs under the slave system. (Rex, 1970: 54.)

While there is much in the domestic servant's situation which is suggestive of slavery, this study suggests that domestic servants are most accurately to be viewed as trapped workers. They are trapped in a condition of subjugation and immobility within which they are subject to intensive exploitation.

Such exploitation is evident in their low wages, which ensure physical survival, but little more; their long working hours and lack of paid holidays; their deprivation of family and social life; their low status, lack of job satisfaction; unsatisfactory relationships with their employers; absence of legal protection; and lack of collective bargaining and worker rights. This objective exploitation is expressed in the workers' sense of being slaves, of relative deprivation, of leading wasted lives which they are powerless to change.

Their dependence on their employers is total. The next chapter will attempt to show what kind of women these employers are. In his novel *Vanity Fair*, Thackeray states that 'the worst tyrants over women are [other] women'. Certainly the institution of domestic service allows a measure of domestic tyranny; however it is not individuals this study is attacking. These domestic 'tyrants' are also, in a very real sense, victims of structures.

6 The Employers

Two women placed together makes cold weather.
Shakespeare, Henry VIII, *Act I Scene 4*

My standpoint . . . can less than any other make the
individual responsible for relations whose creature he
remains, socially speaking, however much he may
subjectively raise himself above them.
Marx, Preface to Capital

There is a sense in which this is a study in the politics of
dependence. While the key to understanding the domestic worker's
situation is her dependence on her employer, the employer is
frequently in an extremely dependent situation herself.

The employers in the sample covered a wide range of class positions,
ages, educational attainments and aspirations, occupational roles,
experiences and attitudes, family arrangements and life-styles. This
heterogeneous group showed three common characteristics: all were
English-speaking, which is predominantly true of the sample area.
Many of the employers interviewed, and all of the farmers' wives in the
study, are descended from or related to the 1820 Settlers. This is true of
myself as well and was an important point of contact in the interview
situation. All of them acknowledge their British ancestry and traditions
with some pride. This is 'Settler Country' par excellence. All were
whites, and this partly defined the sampling frame. All enjoyed a fairly
high standard of living, as do most whites in South Africa today. The
majority (84 per cent) live in the two urban areas in the sample,
Grahamstown and Port Alfred, the remaining 16 per cent on farms.

Some of its white inhabitants see this area as Thomas Gray saw
Grasmere, 'a little unsuspected paradise, where all is peace, rusticity
and happy poverty'. Grahamstown is noted for its cathedral, its
famous schools, tree-lined streets, white-washed 'Settler' homes, the

1820 Settler Monument, and its 'English' atmosphere.[1] The white area presents a sharp contrast to the black township, marked as it is by extreme poverty, slum housing, overcrowding, eroded roads, overflowing refuse bins, and noise.

The other urban area in the district investigated, Port Alfred, is noted for its golf course, seventeen miles of navigable river, beautiful lagoons and swimming beaches. It is a popular holiday resort accommodating something of the order of 5000 visitors every Christmas in its various hotels, holiday homes, caravan and camping sites. Its black township is noted for its extreme poverty and poor housing. The contrast between white and black living conditions is amplified by their physical proximity.

The whites' standard of living in the area must be located in the context of the high standard of living of whites generally in South Africa today. In 1970 the median income of white families was £1258 with an average family size of 3.7 persons. In Grahamstown, Willsworth has calculated that 81.3 per cent of the white population earned more than £660; 63.3 per cent more than £1000; and 4.7 per cent earned plus £3300.[2] Since 1970 most white incomes have, of course, risen.

The majority of the white employer sample, 96 per cent, lived in houses, rather than flats. The sizes of their homes varied a good deal, but most were substantial and on the whole pleasant and comfortably furnished. All the employers owned at least one expensive consumer item such as a television or Hi-fi set or refrigerator, and at least one motor car. The houses ranged from the small, suburban, comfortably furnished dwelling, to extremely luxurious homes set in beautiful gardens with swimming pools, large lawns and colourful flower beds, and furnished with Persian rugs, Sanderson linens and antiques.

The ages of the employers in the sample ranged from 20 to 75. Most were married. The occupations of the husbands showed a considerable range, from university lecturer, doctor, teacher, attorney, estate agent, school teacher, business executive, bookkeeper, museum assistant, commercial salesman, market agent, dentist, pharmacist, shopowner, civil servant, farmer, works supervisor, retired electrical engineer and accountant, to male nurse. The vast majority fall within various gradations of middle-class status as defined by occupation and income.

All the married women in the sample had children. On average each had one child under 16 years of age, and two over 16 years of age. The average household size was 3.3 persons. (This contrasts with an average household size of 6.7 persons among the black domestic worker sample.)

There was a considerable range of educational attainment. Only just over half of the sample had passed Standard Ten. Of the remaining women, sixteen had passed only Standard Eight, and five had passed only Standard Six. However, 64 per cent had some other training or education, such as a secretarial course (14 per cent); nursing (12 per cent); teacher training (8 per cent); while 20 per cent had a university degree. Like their black employees, their educational aspirations for their children were high, though there was an extreme sex differential. While only 20 per cent ideally would choose a profession for their daughters which involved a university education, 60 per cent chose it for their sons.

The great majority of the married women had worked before they were married. The range of jobs covered was that of traditionally female dominated occupations, the largest occupational category being bookkeeping or secretarial work, which covered 38 per cent of the married women in the sample. Others had worked as nurses, florist, sales ladies, teachers and librarian. All had been satisfied with their jobs. The most common reasons they gave for leaving their jobs were to get married and to be with their children, or when they fell pregnant.

Only just over a quarter of the currently married women were employed outside the home, and only one of the widows. All the three women in the employer sample who had never been married were currenly employed. All gave as their reason for continuing to work their need for the monetary income.

Attitudes and Activities

Attitudes towards women working outside the home showed a good deal of variety. Twenty-four per cent of the respondents felt that as a general rule women should work outside the home; 24 per cent thought they should not; and the majority of 52 per cent thought it depended on circumstances. It was frequently stated that mothers with young children should not work. Just over half of the forty-three married women with children thought their children either would suffer or would have suffered if they had worked; 11 per cent thought their children would have benefited, largely from the extra income this would have brought into the family; and the remainder, 36 per cent, thought it depended on circumstances. Many employers fail to realise that their domestic servants are often themselves mothers with young children.

Many stated that women's prime role was a domestic one. Some comments were:

A woman's place is in the home.

A wife's first job is her house and husband.

There is enough valuable work for women to do in the home.

When women work they lose their femininity and get stroppy.
That makes for unhappy marriages.

I had expected to find some divergence between the attitudes of the married women in the sample and those of their husbands towards women working outside the home. But the majority, 84 per cent, said that their husbands had the same view as themselves on this topic. Only 9 per cent said their husbands had different views. Sometimes this was a source of discontent:

I would like to work but my husband won't allow it.

A small number, 7 per cent of the married women, said they did not know their husband's views on this question.

I don't know. We've never discussed it.

The majority of the women interviewed would ideally have liked a part-time job outside the home. Only 26 per cent would ideally have chosen to be housewives, and only 12 per cent would ideally have chosen to be doing a full-time job. Of the fifteen women in the sample presently employed, a third would ideally have preferred to be housewives. The vast majority, 98 per cent, thought most of their friends felt the same way. The only respondent who thought they felt differently ideally chose part-time work for herself, but thought most of her friends would prefer to be housewives.

Many voiced their objections to the fact that there were so few opportunites for part-time work. Several felt strongly that some extra-domestic role was important, not only as a source of income but for social contacts and 'an opportunity to get out of the home'. Some comments from housewives were:

I feel very flat when everyone else goes off to school or to work, and I'm left alone at home (except for the maid).

I feel left behind.

The Home Industries Association, now established in both Grahamstown and Port Alfred, appears to fulfil an important need here, especially among farmers' wives. Several said that their lives seemed fuller and richer and they had 'got to know more people' and 'felt part of things more' through their common involvement in this enterprise. In both towns Home Industries sells home-made produce such as jams and cakes, handcraft products, and fresh fruit and vegetables. The irony here is that in many cases it appears that the domestic workers do most of the baking and cooking of the products offered for sale.

Despite the fact that the majority of women interviewed said they would ideally like a part-time job outside the home, the majority, 80 per cent, also said that they were not bored at home. Only 14 per cent of the women not currently working said they were bored at home, and a small proportion, 6 per cent, said they were bored sometimes. This attitude can perhaps best be understood in terms of the leisure activities they enjoyed which, in sharp contrast to those of their black women employees, were varied, rich and interesting. They were thus in a very different position from housewives in other societies where 'the lack of contact with other people coupled with the almost non-existence of a social life or leisure activities . . . presents a depressing picture . . .' (Hobson, 1978: 87.)

Their level of involvement in voluntary organisations was very high. Over half belonged to voluntary associations such as church groups like the Catholic Women's League, the Methodist Women's Auxiliary and the Anglican Women's Guild. They also belonged to various social and interest groups such as Pistol Clubs, Coomb Social Club, the Bathurst Reading Circle, Diaz Cross Bird Club, the Women's Agricultural Association, the Grahamstown Amateur Dramatic Society, the National Council of Women, Settlers' Club in Grahamstown, Rhodes University Women's Association, the Bathurst Horticultural Society, the Kowie Trust and the Port Alfred and Grahamstown Home Industries Association. In addition several were involved in community work through associations such as the Grahamstown City Council, the Port Alfred Ratepayers' Association, the Society for the Prevention of Cruelty to Animals, Child Welfare, Red Cross, Rotary

Annes, the Bathurst Agricultural Show Committee, school feeding schemes in both towns, the Bathurst and District Welfare Society, and so on. On average each of these women belonged to 2.7 voluntary associations.

The majority, 94 per cent, belonged to a Christian church. The two largest denominations were the Anglican Church, to which 36 per cent of the sample belonged, and the Methodist Church, to which 32 per cent belonged. The frequency with which they attended church varied a good deal: 36 per cent said they went to church two to three times a month, 26 per cent went to church four or more times, 16 per cent once a month and 22 per cent said they went to church 'seldom'. Most of those who said seldom expressed guilt that they did not go more frequently. This contrasts strongly with the regret expressed by many domestic servants that their working hours did not give them the opportunity to go to church more.

Many of the employers said they had regular sporting or social activities such as tennis, golf, bridge and bowls. Several of the older employers said they had enjoyed regular sporting activities when they were younger.

Perhaps not surprisingly, the most lively discussion during the interviews was to do with which two television programmes the employer enjoyed the most. The majority, 66 per cent, spent their evenings watching television. Most employers, 88 per cent, listened to the radio and the majority of these said they listened daily. Most had access to a number of other media. The great majority, 70 per cent, said they read a daily or weekly newspaper. Most of these read the *Eastern Province Herald*. The majority also read one or more magazines, with an average of 2.2 magazines each. The most frequently mentioned were *Fair Lady*, *Scope*, *Farmers' Weekly*, *Your Family* and *The Readers' Digest*.

In addition, 98 per cent said they enjoyed a number of hobbies or special interests such as sewing, knitting, gardening, reading, baking, making jams and preserves, tapestry, painting, drama, tennis, golf, bowls, dressmaking, writing letters, photography, music, singing in a choir, and listening to the radio and watching television. Week-ends were spent on these hobbies and in a variety of other leisure activities such as going to the beach, visiting friends, playing sport or watching their husbands and children doing so, and entertaining. The amount of entertaining varied a good deal; the largest category, 46 per cent, were those who said they entertained only occasionally; 14 per cent said they entertained on average three times a week; and 24 per cent on average once a week, often on week-ends only. Sixteen per cent said they did no entertaining at all.

The vast majority, 92 per cent, took holidays in another place. Of these, 42 per cent said they did the domestic work themselves when they went on holiday; 16 per cent said the family shared the domestic work; and 10 per cent said they usually stayed in a hotel. Almost a third, 32 per cent, said a domestic servant did the domestic work when the family went on holiday, and often this was their own servant. She accompanied them to their holiday house (rented or owned) and this was considered her 'holiday'. In twelve cases this was the usual practice. One employer explained:

She does get an hour or so on the beach in the afternoons.

It seems clear that the employment of domestic workers frees these women, in a number of ways and on a variety of levels, from the constraints their domestic role would otherwise impose.

Relations with Employees

Many employers described their servant as one of the family. This implies that she is seen in a role-specific dimension, that her life is viewed as totally enmeshed with that of her employers. Yet not one of the domestic workers in the sample saw herself as one of the family and some voiced cynicism about their employers' use of this phrase. In no case was there the sharing of power and resources that authentic family membership might be thought to involve.

Relations between domestic workers and white employers in the Eastern Cape study are characterised by various degrees of formality, rigidity, authoritarianism and social distance. Personal interaction is largely limited to the work situation, yet the majority of the employers said they liked their servants as people, and got along well with them. When asked to describe their feelings towards their servants, 30 per cent said they were 'one of the family', and a further 28 per cent said they felt fondness or friendship for their servants. Six per cent described their predominant feeling for their servants as 'pity' and another 6 per cent said their predominant feeling was 'irritation'. Thus while the structure of the worker-employer relationship is extremely hierarchic and unequal, in terms of content it is often coloured for the employer with emotions of kindness, affection and generosity. It is precisely the unequal nature of the relationship and the mutual recognition of such inequality that allows the relationship to be described so often as a close and friendly one.

The pervading tone of interaction does not appear to be one of mistrust, watchfulness or suspicion on the part of the employers. The majority said their servants were trustworthy, five thought they were not, and three said they were not sure. Some commented:

You can never tell with them.

Blacks are all kleptomaniacs nowadays.

Yes, she's trustworthy . . . as far as native girls go.

As much as any of them.

I trust her completely. I never lock anything away.

The employers' answers to the questions 'How would you describe your feelings towards her?' and 'What sort of person is she?' showed a great variety. Some comments were:

She's very raw . . . just out of the kraal.[3]

An impossible thing. Very self-willed. She's the first girl I've had that's gone to school. The difference is fantastic. She insists on doing things her own way. The completely raw ones are better.[4]

She's a raw farm girl. (Said of a woman aged 58.)

She's like a child of ours.

One of the family.

Very clean.

The good old type.

Pleasant and reserved.

She doesn't have much to say, but I prefer them that way.

She's a gem of a girl. (The 'girl' in this case was a middle-aged woman.)

She's very reliable and responsible. She ran the whole house for two months while I was in hospital.

I suppose my main feeling for her is one of aggravation. She is absolutely stupid. Like a child mentally. She needs a lot of supervision.

We have a good understanding. I told her if anything is missing from this house, you are to blame. I told her that when I first employed her and I've had no trouble.

She's a bit cheeky.

We don't talk much. I have no feelings for her really. I haven't made a friend of her. I keep her at a distance.

Raw of course, but we're very fond of her. She's one of the family.

I love her and I think she loves me.

She's a dear old thing.

You must keep them in their place . . . not get too friendly. That's why I don't let her listen to the radio. If we listened to the radio together she'd start getting familiar. Some people make a big mistake . . . they make friends of their servants. Take my neighbour here . . . she lets her servant bath in her bathroom. I think that's shocking.

Quite a good girl. (Said of the mother of six children.)

She's a proper old farm girl. Not at all insolent. A rare thing nowadays.

Our servants are our responsibility. We have to be their doctors, lawyers and do everything for them.

She's all right so long as she doesn't drink out of my cups.

She's a friend. I'm very fond of her.

She's a warm, generous, loving person.

We are both Christians and both women. That gives us a common bond.

We have an easy, relaxed kind of relationship based on mutual trust.

When asked 'What do you think her feelings are towards you?' some answered:

She thinks I'm her mother.

We are her family.

She adores us.

She must be fond of me after fourteen years.

She enjoys working for us.

She's very fond of me and adores the children.

She loves us all.

I'm a mother to her.

I'm like a sister to her.

Completely indifferent. It's very different to the old days.

She's a closed book.

Respect and affection.

She's very happy here. She lacks for nothing.

I don't know. (The servant had been in her employment for fifteen years.)

Some elderly women living alone seem to depend a good deal upon their domestic workers for company. One said plaintively that she feels 'very alone in the world' when her servant goes off at 5 p.m. Another described how she felt nervous living alone with the current spate of burglaries and derived considerable comfort from the fact that her maid 'sits in the kitchen making her grass mats at night, while I sit here [the lounge] sewing'. This illustrates Katzman's insight that 'many mistresses hired servants to fulfil psychological needs independent of the work involved'. (Katzman, 1978: 270.)

When the employers were asked 'What quality do you like the most about your servant?' some answered:

Her sense of humour.

She's prepared to do anything.

Twenty people can walk in here and she'll produce dinner for them without any grumbling.

Her loyalty.

Her happy nature.

She's steady and honest . . . the old-fashioned type.

If you say lunch for seven at 12.30 it's there.

Very willing and obedient.

She's open. I feel we understand each other.

She's quick and efficient.

Very civil.

Quiet and retiring.

She never gets cross.

She loves the children.

She comes to work whether it rains or storms.

She's very clean . . . one of the old type.

She's very polite. After she gets a phone call she comes to tell me who it was from, what it's about and to say thank you.

She's very good with children. She brought all mine up.

Quite a good girl . . . she doesn't answer back.

Very willing . . . she works in the garden as well.

Polite . . . not cheeky at all.

She's a smiling, happy person.

When asked what quality employers liked the least about their servants, some said:

She has a tendency to get depressed . . . she's not a happy worker.

She smells. (When the researcher asked this farmer's wife whether she had access to water at home, the reply was 'I don't suppose so . . . the dam is quite far away.')

She can sulk.

Her movements are too quick . . . she breaks things.

She's inclined to be rough with my crockery.

Her sourness . . . an unwillingness to be corrected.

She insists on wearing shoes in the house and I find the noise very irritating.

She sometimes comes late in the mornings.

She hurries through her work on Sundays.

I wish she'd talk to my youngest more so he could learn Xhosa.

A lack of thoroughness.

She boozes a bit . . . I've told her it must stop.

She's a slow worker.

'Laziness' was frequently mentioned here. For instance.

She's lazy . . . she sweeps the dust under the carpet.

This is paradoxical in view of the amount of work domestic workers appear to get through in many households. Laziness of course is a common trait in racist stereotypes generally, and especially in colonial societies.[5]

These women's relationships with their servants must be located in a tangled skein of attitudes towards blacks generally. Here, a technique of depersonalisation often operates, a technique Memmi has termed the 'mark of the plural. The colonized is never characterized in an individual manner; he is entitled only to drown in an anonymous collectivity.' Relations with the individual servants are submerged in this impersonal racial sea.

If a colonized servant does not come in one morning, the colonizer will not say that she is ill, or that she is cheating, or that she is tempted not to abide by an oppressive contract. He will say, 'You can't count on them.' It is not just a grammatical expression. He refuses to consider personal, private occurrences in his maid's life; that life in a specific sense does not interest him, and his maid does not exist as an individual. (Memmi, 1974: 85.)

The extent of this depersonalisation is illustrated by the fact that only 10 per cent of the employer sample knew their servants' full Xhosa names. Several habitually called their servants by standardised names, such as 'Cookie' or 'Sissie'.

Overall, employers do not know as much about their servants as their length of employment might warrant. The majority, 84 per cent, knew whether their servant was married or not. Most, 82 per cent, also knew how many children their servants had, and 62 per cent knew roughly how old the children were. Only 40 per cent knew what level of schooling their servant had and 44 per cent did not know whether or not she had children attending school. The vast majority, 82 per cent, did not know the cost of black children's schooling. Overall, only two employers of those who knew their servants had school-going children knew the cost involved.

Less than half of those with live-out servants knew where they lived, and three-quarters of the employers did not know how much rent their servants had to pay. The vast majority, 80 per cent, communicated with their servants in English and found their knowledge of English 'satisfactory'. One employer commented here:

It's too good. We find her reading anything we leave lying around.

Only 12 per cent said they had difficulty communicating with their servants.

Of a total of thirty-one out of the forty-six employers who knew their servants had young children, 67 per cent did not know who looked after the children while she was at work, and most of these did not know whether or not she had to pay anyone to look after her children. Half the employers said their servants discussed their personal problems with them, though only 16 per cent said this was reciprocal. Some commented:

I don't want to know too much.

I don't want to get involved.

We're not at all intimate.

While the pattern of interaction between employers and their servants clearly varies a good deal, the employers' ignorance of their servants' lives and identities outside the work situation is surprising. This is especially so in view of the physical proximity of servant and employer in the workplace.

While the great majority, 98 per cent, said they were satisfied with their present servant, they were sharply critical of servants in general.

The prevalent view was that they are incompetent workers, who are well-treated by their long-suffering employers. The subordinate status of the servant was unquestioned: servants are like children. The qualities most commonly attributed to them are irresponsibility, secretiveness, an inability to work without close supervision, laziness, dishonesty, ingratitude and a lack of initiative. In short, they are indubitably inferior.

Attitudes towards Domestic Workers

Most employers, 60 per cent, thought that on the whole domestic servants as a group are 'well treated'. Other opinions ranged from 8 per cent who thought servants as a group were exceptionally well treated, 10 per cent who thought they were badly treated, 6 per cent who thought they were treated only satisfactorily, and 16 per cent who thought that the treatment of domestic servants varied too much to be able to generalise. Some commented:

You can only get so much out of them and no more.

They take no pride in their work.

In Rhodesia a boy does three times the work these do.

Servants are treated too well. That's the trouble. They don't want to work.

You never see any thin servants.

A girl in a good home in Grahamstown is extremely well off. She gets good pay, food and clothing.

They give what they get.

No, employers expect far too much from them. They forget that their girls are also people.

I can only speak from my own experience. I treat my girl well and so do most of my friends.

Yes, we pay good wages.

It's really wonderful that they're willing to work for such low wages.

They're well treated. Some are filthy, lazy and unreliable . . . especially those from across the (Fish) river.

Port Alfred servants are very bad, especially the young ones. I had eight in my first year here . . . they're dirty and unreliable.

They're well treated, considering what poor workers they are.

They're treated as well as servants anywhere, but there's room for improvement.

It varies a great deal. Some treat them like they're one of the family. But a friend of mine has had forty maids in five years. It varies a lot.

They are taken too much for granted.

They're usually treated as one of the family.

This is a political question. I'd rather not answer political questions. Our government is given to us by God.

Some employers I know lack compassion towards their servants. They work them at Christmas and Easter and let them walk home late at night.

They're well treated, especially as they are not good workers. They're very deceitful on the whole.

Black people now are more difficult to get on with. They're becoming more demanding and therefore more irritating to employers.

Farm natives are unreliable. They have no interest in their work . . . most employers here have endless trouble, especially those who do the most for their natives.

Servants here are shocking. A lot of farmers are selling up because of staff problems. In the old days the youngsters were given a jolly good hiding if they did something wrong. Now parents seem to be afraid of their children.

The question 'What could be done to improve the situation of domestic servants?' often provoked a lot of complaints about servants generally:

Everyone is complaining about their increasing cheekiness.

They don't take any pride in their employers' houses.

Only one employer mentioned the need for more jobs and four the need for better pay:

I get hot under the collar when I hear what people pay.

Another employer believed that more training for servants was necessary, and three thought they should be better treated by their employers:

Employers should realise that servants are people, not animals.

Overall, attitudes towards domestic servants in the Eastern Cape may be categorised into five main types:

'Embarrassment'. A small number feel embarrassed at having any servants at all, and think that being waited on by another human being is degrading. Many of these make small gestures towards self-reliance such as washing their own underwear.

'Moral responsibility'. An equally small number feel that one has a moral obligation to provide employment to blacks through the institution of domestic service. They express considerable concern over black poverty and give generously to local charities:

'A necessary evil'. A small proportion 'just cannot keep a servant'. Several respondents in the sample reported this about various neighbours. They find fault with everything their servants do, nag them constantly, and are generally antagonistic to blacks.

'One of the family'. These employers pride themselves on their 'luck' in having such good servants, say they are one of the family and have employed them for many years. They look after their servants when they are sick and allow them favours such as watching television in the lounge.

'I know the native'. These employers often know their servants' language. They think they understand 'the native' well and appreciate their traditional customs. They are patient, willing to overlook minor faults in their servants' work and treat them, in their view, kindly but firmly. They are critical of those who 'spoil' servants.

The most typical viewpoint is that servants are like children. Thus, the core characteristic of the relationship is a paternalism which involves a dependence on the part of the servant and confirms the employer's sense of superiority. Certainly these women do not see themselves as exploiters. A press report on this research provoked some resentful letters addressed to me personally, one of which specifically stated, 'I resent being called an exploiter.'

Inside the Home

It is important to recognise that domestic servants are a deeply entrenched part of the white South African life-style. (At the present time, in 1988, two out of three white households employ a domestic servant, according to the Central Statistical Services report cited in the *Star*, 24.3.1988.) All the employers in the sample employed a domestic servant, on either a full-time or a part-time basis. In the widespread employment of domestic servants, contemporary white South African society resembles the Stuart period of English history where, as Laslett points out, 'a quarter or a third of all the families in the country contained servants . . . and this meant that very humble people had them as well as the titled and the wealthy'. (Laslett, 1965: 12.)

Of course this changed, and by Victorian times the employment of domestic servants was the prerogative of the upper and middle classes. The large family, the large, over-furnished house, the entertainment of guests at lavish dinner parties and large functions,

> all of which were essential attributes of the institution of the Victorian middle class family, required the employment of domestic servants on a vast scale. By their number, dress and function they proclaimed in an outward and visible way, the degree of success in life that their employer had attained. (Burnett, 1977: 136.)

While this may still be true of the larger urban centres in South Africa, in the Eastern Cape study most households employed only one domestic servant.[6] The predominant pattern here appears to be the 'maid of all work'. Most employers, 92 per cent, said their servants did general domestic work, while only 8 per cent were employed in specialised roles such as washing, cooking or ironing.

Given the traditional connection between the employment of servants and the white 'South African way of life', the employment of servants does not generally confer status on their employers. However, a considerable amount of labour-time goes into feeding the employer's family, and into the provision of services which may enable him or her to live in a style which indicates a high social position. Such services include waiting at table at elaborate dinner parties, and serving coffee to bridge guests at a late hour.

Servants are obtained in three main ways: through recommendation by a friend of the employer (32 per cent of the employer sample obtained their present servant through this route); recommendation by the previous servant (14 per cent); and through domestic servants coming to the employers' door and asking for work (18 per cent).

Most employers had had the same domestic servants for several years. The length of employment of their current servant ranged from two months to thirty-seven years, and included, in addition to the servant with thirty-seven years' service, one who had worked for the same employer for thirty-two years and another for thirty years. The average length of service with their present employer was seven years. One employer who had had her present servant for thirteen years and her previous one for forty-nine years pointed out that her servant's mother and two sisters had together served the family for just over 100 years.

Over a third of employers, 38 per cent, had dismissed their previous servant. One farmer's wife said, 'My husband sacked the whole family.' Other reasons were:

She was playing up.

She went off her head so I got rid of her. (This woman had worked for her employer for forty years.)

She was sacked for stealing.

I sacked her when she got sour.

I sacked her because she became a hypochondriac. (After twelve years' service.)

She got spoilt. She was demanding more and more and doing less and less, so I got rid of her.

I sacked her for cheekiness. I've had to sack many for this.

She was sacked for not playing the game.

I had to sack the last three because they got pregnant.

Only in 22 per cent of the cases had the servant left the job of her own choice.

She did a bunk in the night the way they often do.

She walked out. She said she didn't want to work on Sundays. She said she had to go to church and feed her own children. She didn't think about us.

She died just after she left me after fifty years' service.

The amount of domestic work actually done by the employers themselves varied. A fairly large proportion, 20 per cent, said they did no domestic work at all themselves, and 12 per cent said they did 'very little'. In one case this seemed to involve only 'tidying drawers'. Another mentioned 'baking cakes occasionally' and another: 'I make our bed. I don't fancy letting them do it . . . they're too dirty.' However, 44 per cent said they enjoyed domestic work.

Most of them saw themselves as solely responsible for the organisation of the home. The involvement of their husbands in domestic organisation was often fairly minimal. Just over 60 per cent of the married respondents said their husbands never helped with the domestic work. Only 19 per cent said their husbands helped regularly, and 21 per cent said their husbands helped occasionally. I expected to find a considerable generational difference in the involvement of men in domestic work, but this was not borne out by the research. Sixty-one per cent of the married women said their husbands were very similar to their fathers in this respect. However, 30 per cent said their husbands helped in the house more than their fathers had done. Nine per cent said their husbands helped less.

This role differentiation is sometimes at variance with the women's own attitudes. The majority of the married women (62 per cent) thought that men should help in the house; 6 per cent thought that there was no general rule, that the degree men should be involved in domestic work depended entirely on the family situation; 32 per cent thought this was definitely a woman's sphere and men should not help in the house at all. I often had the impression that the respondents had not thought about this question before, since their answers often involved a good deal of hesitation and uncertainty. It was also very apparent that the role of servants is a pivotal aspect of this question. Several commented:

Men should help if there are no servants. On farms here we usually have lots of servants, so it's not necessary.

Other comments were:

Yes, occasionally he should cut himself a slice of bread or pull up a chair.

Men should help occasionally with little things.

No, men get under your feet in the kitchen.

Yes, he'll do unusual things like pour the tea out but he won't make it. He's never made tea in his life.

I don't know. We've never discussed it.

Yes, why should a man sit from 12 p.m. on Saturday until Monday morning when the wife can't sit down for a minute? I don't expect him to put on an apron though.

I don't know . . . my husband was the only son. He was never taught to help in the house.

No, men have got their own work to do.

Yes . . . I think so . . . younger people expect more of their husbands today.

No, men would get in the way.

Nice if they do, but we shouldn't expect it.

No, men have to cope with tension at work. They need to relax when they get home.

Why shouldn't men help with the housework? Some people think the man is a king in the household and treat him like a visitor. At least men should help with the heavy work.

No, I don't like a man to be a sissy.

It's changing now . . . in the past when we had umpteen servants men did nothing in the house. Now men should give you a hand sometimes if you have no maid.

The employers interviewed gave a great range of reasons for employing a domestic servant. Of two who said it was for 'security reasons', one said, 'I don't feel safe on my own during the day,' and the other, 'I'm on my own here so I have to have someone to sleep in.' Others said:

So I can give my children all the attention they need.

It means I can go out. When I go out my husband is looked after. Otherwise I'd be completely tied down.

I work for Home Industries. I need help with making jams and cakes.

To give me more free time.

To give me more time to look after my children.

I couldn't manage without . . . we haven't got electricity.

To run the house and look after the children while I'm at work.

I hate housework, it's never finished.

It frees me to do things of more value like needlework and dressmaking.

It makes life easier.

For health reasons . . . I have diabetes and arthritis.

I teach and so she does everything. She gets the children up in the morning, gives them their breakfast, walks the youngest to nursery school, has our lunch ready for us when we return . . . everything really.

It frees me to work in the Advice Office and do other useful things in the community.

Housework is monotonous . . . you don't achieve anything.

I don't know . . . I couldn't imagine not having a servant.

To help her out. She's got seven children.

My husband doesn't like me to scrub the floors and do heavy work.

I would prefer to be independent and do my own work. I only keep four because I feel sorry for them.

I would prefer one servant who earned R40 a month (about £13.30). But they don't want that . . . they prefer to be part of a group. (Employer of three servants.)

I have a vast home and four sons. I'd be a martyr to the house if I didn't have servants.

I couldn't manage without.

Altogether 30 per cent said they could not manage to run their homes without a domestic servant.

Wages

Although all the 225 households in the sample employed domestic servants, only 22 per cent employed live-in servants. The majority of employers said their servants started work early in the morning. For 50 per cent of them this meant between 6 and 7 a.m., and for 42 per cent between 7 and 8 a.m. The hours at which they stopped work for the day showed more variation, with 24 per cent stopping at 2 p.m., 22 per cent at 5 p.m., 28 per cent between 3 and 4 p.m. and 10 per cent at 8 p.m. Just over half the employers said their servants had some time off during the day, though one employer said this was only 'for going to the toilet'. The worst case started work at 6 a.m. and went off around 9 p.m. six nights a week.

Over a quarter of the employers' servants, according to their account, worked less than a 40-hour week, and may thus be considered part-time workers. Their working week ranged from thirty-nine to three hours. The full-time workers' week ranged from forty-two to eighty-four working hours with an average of 57.9 working hours a week.

The majority of the employers of live-out servants, 52 per cent, did not know how long their employees spent travelling to and from work. Seven said their servants spent about half an hour; three said they spent between half to one hour; and three said one to two hours. Of the thirty-nine employers in this category, twenty-five said their servants walked to and from work, and fourteen said they travelled by bus.

Less than half the thirty-six employers of full-time servants gave their servants one day off each week. Twenty-two per cent said their servants got no day off; 11 per cent said their servants got a half day off; 14 per cent gave their servants one and a half days off; and 8 per cent gave their servants two days off a week.

The great majority of employers required their domestic servants to work on public holidays. Only 12 per cent said their servants did not have to work on public holidays.

In her Durban study, Preston-Whyte reported that 'all employers acknowledged that their servants should have a holiday each year'. (Preston-Whyte, 1969: 108.) In the Eastern Cape study the majority of the employers, 68 per cent, said their servants were given an annual holiday. Yet the situation is ambiguous. As noted earlier, twelve employers said they took their servants with them to their holiday house on the coast. This they define as their 'holiday'. The servants, of course, have a different definition. In several other cases the servant had to come to work to water pot plants, air the house or feed pets while her employer was away on holiday. This situation is similarly open to different definitions on the part of employers and servants. Because of a suspicion that a 'lie factor' may have been operating here, the employers' answers have not been included in the overall calculations.[7]

In addition it is possible that employers were sometimes lying about working hours: in five cases the servant was present later than the time at which that employer said she stopped work (for example, one served tea at 4.30 p.m. but was said to stop work at 2 p.m.); sometimes about uniforms (in three cases the employer said the servant was supplied with a uniform but the servant was observed not wearing one); in addition to which the question on wages was often answered defensively: once the employer got up to close the door between the lounge and the dining room where the servant was working, before answering.

According to the employers' responses, sixteen gave their servants two weeks' annual holiday; eleven gave three weeks; six gave one week; and one employer gave her servant six weeks holiday a year. Ninety-one per cent of the thirty-four employers who gave their servants an annual holiday said they paid them during this period.[8]

The general pattern seems to be to give the servant some time off on Christmas Day. Twenty-six employers said their servants spent some of Christmas Day with their own families; eight said it varied; but sixteen said their servants spent none of Christmas Day with their own families.

Wages

According to the employers, the average wage paid to full-time workers (who numbered thirty-six plus one woman who refused to answer this question) was £8.31 a month. The average cash wage paid to full-time workers calculated from the domestic servants' responses was lower – £7.82.

Less than half (40 per cent) of the employers decided to pay this amount themselves; 28 per cent said their husbands decided; and

32 per cent said that they and their husbands had decided together. Only in 10 per cent of the sample had there been any discussion between the employer and the domestic worker over the starting wage. Sometimes this was of a surprising nature. For example, one employer who was asked 'How was your starting wage arrived at?' replied:

I asked her how much she wanted. She said R10 a month and I said that was too little. (Employer pays R13 a month, about £4.30.)

Fifty-eight per cent said their current wage was not the servants' starting wage; however 42 per cent said it was. In only 10 per cent of the cases was this wage increased annually. The remaining twenty-four employers who had increased their servants' wages said they did so irregularly.

Many employers were somewhat shamefaced about the wages they paid and were eager to point out the amount they paid in kind. These payments were not as large or comprehensive as I had expected. For example, while all employers provided at least one meal a day, the quantity and quality of food given seem to vary a good deal. Six per cent of the employers provided only breakfast, usually mealie meal porridge, or bread and jam with tea. Sixty-four per cent provided lunch and breakfast, one provided lunch only, and 28 per cent provided all meals. Lunch often consisted of mealie meal or samp, beans and other vegetables and, in a small proportion of cases, meat.

Eighteen per cent gave both servants' rations and food from their own table, which was often, but not invariably, 'left-overs' that would otherwise have been thrown away. One employer commented, 'I don't like to throw anything away so I give it to her rather.'

Another said, 'I give her what the dogs wouldn't like.' Thirty-eight per cent gave their servants the same food as they ate themselves, and 44 per cent gave servants' rations only. Forty per cent said they gave their servants no meat at all. Eighteen per cent said they gave their servants meat once a week; 12 per cent gave 'servants' meat' daily; 28 per cent gave their servants the same meat they ate themselves either daily or almost daily, and one gave 'servants' meat' three times a week.

Despite the fact that 40 per cent of the employers gave their servants no meat at all, the great majority, 94 per cent, consider that they provide servants with a balanced diet. The juxtaposition of these two figures would be less surprising if employers provided their servants with other sources of protein such as fish or eggs, but in no case was this done. Obviously, what the employers consider a balanced diet for their servants is very different from what they would consider adequate for themselves. This double standard is a familiar theme in the literature on blacks in South Africa generally. Two of the employers were remarkable for their candour in admitting that they did not provide their servants with a balanced diet, and another said she had not thought about it.

The majority, 96 per cent, said their servants were satisfied with the food they received. But only 16 per cent of the domestic servants interviewed said they were satisfied with the quantity and quality of their food. Most employers (78 per cent) rationed the quantity of food given while others did not and simply trusted the servant to help herself to a reasonable amount. The majority of the thirty-nine employers of live-out servants (77 per cent) allowed them to take food home. Though most employers, 72 per cent, said they only provided sufficient food to feed the servant herself, the remainder said they provided enough to feed some of her family as well as herself. The majority of the employers, 62 per cent, thought their servants did not ever take food without asking; 32 per cent thought they sometimes did, and 6 per cent said they didn't know.

Most of the employers (82 per cent) said they provided their servants with a uniform, though this was sometimes only an apron. Seventy-two per cent said they also provided their servants with other clothing, usually their own or their family's old clothing. Another 28 per cent either gave their servants no other clothing or else they sold their old clothing to them. Some commented:

It's better to charge them. Then they appreciate it more.

I never give them anything which I cannot use.

Yes, I used to give her overalls. But she said they were pinched off the washing line. I think she sold them to get money for drink.

Anything that's too old and shabby for me, she gets.

I give her old clothing rather than throw things away. I hate waste . . . but I must say I often cut things up for floor cloths.

The majority of employers, 76 per cent, said they provided medicines for their employees when they were ill. Some paid the fee for them to visit the clinic, and in a few cases the employers paid doctors' bills as well. Children's schooling expenses, a major item of expense in most black families' budgets, were contributed towards on a regular basis by only 4 per cent of the employers. Eighty-eight per cent said they did not contribute and 8 per cent said the question was not applicable as they were certain their servant did not have children attending school.

Some employers also provided access to other resources including the use of the telephone, the use of a radio and occasionally the privilege of watching television with the family, the use of the stove to cook for herself or her family, a room in the case of live-in servants, and the use of the employer's facilities to do her own or her family's laundry. Employers seem sometimes to be quite unaware of the difficulty they impose upon their servants when the latter facility is denied. One Bathurst employer whose laundry is done in the washing machine by her live-in servant makes the servant send her own washing home to her mother in Bathurst location. It is laundered in the weed-filled pond at the side of the road into the town. Some farm wokers are given milk, 'damaged fruit' and the use of a plot to grow vegetables. Only in one case in the farm-employers investigated were the workers allowed to graze a limited number of stock, but that meant that they lost the bonus paid to those who had no stock.

Domestic workers have three other possible sources of cash income besides their wages: overtime pay, tips from guests, and Christmas presents. In this sample the amounts paid were very small. Only 12 per cent of the employers said they paid overtime for work done outside of normal hours; half said they did not pay overtime; and 38 per cent said the question was not applicable as their servants never worked overtime. Twenty per cent said they paid their servants extra if there were guests in the house; 62 per cent said they did not – though it was often mentioned that they expected their guests to tip, and 18 per cent said they never had guests to stay. The majority, 60 per cent, gave extra money at Christmas. The gifts ranged from £10 to 30p.

Over half (56 per cent) of the entire sample said they gave Christmas presents other than cash. Christmas gifts commonly consist of their food or clothing or both. Of the twenty-eight employers who gave Christmas presents, nineteen gave food. This varied from a packet of sweets to a fairly substantial box of groceries. Four employers gave clothing, sometimes their own clothing, sometimes new articles; three gave both food and clothing; one gave her servant a dress length; one gave a towel, soap and a washchoth. Another gave 'a petticoat and a towel'. Sometimes the servant's uniform constituted her Christmas present.

Other sources of cash income are exceptional. Only one employer in the sample pays into a savings account for her servant and only one had any kind of pension scheme. One employer commented:

I try to keep them young.

A small number of employers deduct from their servants' wages in the case of illness (three cases) and for breakages (one). When asked 'Do you deduct breakages from her pay?' one employer replied with a good deal of self-satisfaction:

No . . . I don't have any. I've worked out a way of coping with that. The first time she chips a plate or a cup I call her out to the stoep. I take that plate or cup and tell her to watch. I then drop it on the cement floor so it smashes. Then I deduct the cost from her pay. You only have to do it once.

There was a stunned silence from me, the interviewer, who for once was at a loss and unable to offer the usual smiles (albeit strained) and nods of assent to whatever her informant was saying. The informant continued:

You have to do it. Otherwise they chip things on purpose because then they think you will give it to them. You only have to do it once.

When asked, 'What do you do when your servant does something wrong or badly?' most employers said they reprimanded her.

I give her hell.

I get annoyed . . . often it's because I'm upset about something else and I'm letting off steam.

The extent to which employers controlled their servants' work routines and contacts varied a good deal. Visitors to the domestic servant at her place of work seem generally to be discouraged. Sixty-four per cent did not allow members of their servant's family to visit her at work, and 70 per cent did not allow friends or other servants in the neighbourhood to do so. But when asked 'Do you think she ever feels lonely during the day?' all the employers said 'No'.

These data suggest that the white employers in the sample exploit their domestic servants. The employment of domestic servants frees them from a great many of the constraints of their domestic roles, and enables them to engage in a variety of social and occupational activities and interests outside the home. The importance of domestic servants in these women's lives is not reflected in the way they are treated, especially not in the wages they are paid, both in cash and in kind, and the long working hours and arduous duties expected of them. While the domestic servant's dependence on her employer is considerable, her employer is frequently in an extremely dependent situation herself. She is often the 'victim' of an increasingly authoritarian society in which all relations are hierarchically defined, and specifically of a set of attitudes and structures which maintain all women in a subordinate position. Even so, the relationship between black and white women within the institution of domestic service presents a challenge to any feminist notion of 'sisterhood'.

The Employers as Wives

These employers frequently have a rather nebulous power in the home. Although that majority of the currently married informants, 65 per cent, know what their husbands' income is, a surprisingly high proportion of 35 per cent said they did not know. When asking this question I stressed that I was not going to ask what that income was, but simply whether they had access to the information or not. Financial arrangements varied a good deal. Almost one third of the currently married women among the employers said their husbands gave them a regular allowance; the same number said they had to ask their husbands for money whenever they wanted it for any reason. In four cases the wives themselves controlled the family income; in six cases there was a joint bank account from which the wife could draw freely and five employers did not want to talk about financial arrangements. Some comments were:

He gives me pocket money if he's not short.

He gives me my housekeeping allowance in pineapples which I sell at Home Industries.

He never lets me look at his books. I've never been able to find out his income. I have to ask him for money. (A farmer's wife.)

I should have taken more interest in money from the beginning. I have never been able to find out his income. If I had, I could have organised my life better. As it is, he never lets me see his books. (A farmer's wife.)

Of the eleven currently married women who were employed outside the home, 73 per cent said the money they earned was their own so far as their husbands were concerned; they could decide what to do with it. All these women said they spent the money they earned largely on the household. One commented:

What I earn has become the housekeeping money. We don't quarrel about it but now and again I would like something of my own.

The majority of the married women in the sample, 60 per cent, said their husbands made all the financial decisions in their household. Twenty-eight per cent said they shared the financial decision-making with their husbands, and 12 per cent said they made most of the financial decisions themselves.

When asked, 'If you wanted to increase your servant's wages what would you do?' almost half of the married women said they would ask their husbands to do so, three said they would do so and inform their husbands, sixteen said they would discuss it with their husbands and come to a joint decision, and three said they would do so out of the housekeeping money and not tell their husbands.

When asked, 'Who decided to buy or rent this particular home?' 49 per cent of the presently married women said their husbands did so; in one case the wife decided herself; and in 49 per cent of the cases the husband and wife decided together. In the vast majority of cases the title deed of the home is in the husband's name – 88 per cent.

The really significant fact in all this is that when asked, 'Overall, do you feel you have enough say in things to do with the household and family life?' the vast majority (91 per cent) of the currently married women in the sample answered 'Yes'. Many of these women clearly define their role in purely domestic terms. For example:

The husband is the breadwinner. Therefore it's right that he makes all the decisions about money.

Yes, I'm not frightened of him.

Yes, my husband never interferes in anything to do with the housekeeping.

The household is mine . . . I think so. I'm never interfered with unless I don't mend his clothes or serve food he doesn't like. But everything I do is for him. Especially over the hunting season. I slave for two months so he can enjoy himself. But if I want to go to East London and buy plants at the nursery, it doesn't happen.

Another said, in a whisper:

I would like to have more say with money matters.

These responses have to be located in the context of the subjective meanings these women attach to sex, race and class. Their feelings about themselves, as women and as whites, and their feelings about the difference in living conditions between blacks and whites generally in South Africa reflect a cultural order that is intensely patriarchal and race-supremacist.

Almost a quarter of the employers believe that women are generally inferior to men in their personal qualities. Seventy-five per cent thought they were not inferior, and one did not know. This contrasts with the views of the women domestic servants in the sample, only 16 per cent of whom thought that women are generally inferior to men in personal qualities. Some comments were:

Men are better balanced. Women are too emotional and bitchy to each other.

A woman is a womb – her primary function is to be a good mother.

The man should be the head of the family.

One woman dropped her voice, presumably so that her husband sitting in the next room could not overhear:

Between you and me we're equal mentally. Though we do have different viewpoints . . . we look at things differently.

Others said:

Women today seem to be doing a lot in the world. Whether it's good or bad I can't say. But one thing I do know, men should always have the final say.

We lack something. We can't do the top jobs.

We're different. We've got our jobs and they've got theirs.

Yes, women are less intelligent.

No, we're equal, but a man should stay boss.

A woman shouldn't outdo a man.

We're equal but some women make a big mistake in trying to demonstrate how equal they are. Our role is as homemakers.

Women are superior. We work harder than men.

No, but a woman needs a man to look after her and protect her.

We're equal, but we must keep our femininity.

No, but the husband must always have the final say.

No, we're equal. I dont feel inferior to my husband, but he's the head of the family.

Yes, women are different. We can't cope in a man's world.

Yes, the man should be the ruler in the house. Women shouldn't wear the trousers.

Yes, our submission to men is God's law.

While five said they did not know whether women were treated fairly in South Africa, the majority (62 per cent) were sure that they were. Some said:

Yes, all the women I know are fairly happy.

I've been treated fairly . . . I've no complaints.

Yes, women are spoilt in this country.

Yes, women have an easy time here compared to overseas, because we all have servants. (An English immigrant.)

Yes, South African men are much better than English ones. They like to be with their friends in the pub until 8 or 9 p.m. It's lonely. Here the men come home earlier.

Those 28 per cent who thought women are not fairly treated mentioned a number of instances such as sexist attitudes, unequal pay, and lack of access to abortion:

> I've heard that women don't get equal pay for the same work.

> It's a woman's right to decide on abortion.

> When you marry in community of property you lose control of your own affairs.

> In this family we all know that what he (husband) says is law.

> Men think they are superior. We are treated as inferiors . . . as lesser people. We are pushed down and domineered. Men make all the decisions. Decisions should be shared . . . women should have more say. I've got a very domineering husband. Women are not listened to . . . their wants are completely ignored. I'm treated like an imbecile child and I resent it terribly.

> A man would be paid double what I am paid.

> Attitudes which put women down.

> This is a strongly male chauvinist society. The predominant feeling is that women should stay at home while their husbands go off and play rugby all day and get drunk afterwards.

While the Women's Liberation Movement has received fairly wide coverage in recent years in the magazines and newspapers these women often read, 14 per cent had not heard of it. Only three in the entire sample gave a positive response to the Women's Liberation Movement, and one qualified her answer:

> It's a good thing I suppose, but I don't think too much about it.

Most thought it was 'kinky', extremist ('they go too far') or the preserve of frustrated women. They said:

> It's a lot of frustrated women who either haven't been able to get a man, or else they can't keep him.

> A lot of nonsense.

> I don't know much about it and I don't want to know any more.

All the women I know are already liberated.

I'm totally opposed to it. Women are castrating men. It's against God's will.

I'm not a Women's Libber . . . there are differences.

I don't believe in demonstrating and trying to prove you are equal.

I'm satisfied to carry on as I've always carried on.

Perhaps I'm old-fashioned but I don't agree with it.

One woman married to a wealthy farmer, who has a beautiful home, a regular clothing allowance and who takes frequent overseas trips, commented:

My life is too good for me to want to join them.

Others said:

A lot of frustrated women . . . fortunately I'm not one of them.

There's no need to shout so loud.

They're too aggressive.

There's no need for all this fuss. Women are equal in our house.

Pshaw . . . I don't like to see girls without bras.

They're going about things the wrong way. Women mustn't try and demonstrate that they are the same as men. They throw away their assets and influence by doing so.

Clearly the majority of these women accept their subordinate position in society. They are trapped in an ideology of domesticity which accepts as natural and inevitable the relations of male domination and female subordination.

The majority of these women are also 'domestic workers'. Many of them are separated not only from the means of production, but also from the means of exchange. They are therefore dependent upon the redistribution of their husbands' wage, which is conducted in private between them. Their position thus involves an economic dependence.[9] Bell and Newby suggest that such dependence promotes deference.

They argue that 'the relationship between husband and wife is a deferential one in that is traditionally-legitimated and hierarchical. It appears both natural and immutable.' 'Deference stabilizes the hierarchical nature of the husband-wife relationship' which 'is embedded in a system of power'. (Bell and Newby, 1976: 164.) This power is moral and physical as well as economic. Thus both domestic servants and their employers are in a dependent situation, and the employers are themselves caught up in a different dimension of 'the deferential dialectic'. The difference between paid and unpaid domestic work is reflected in the differing consciousness of the two types of domestic worker. The paid domestic worker is dependent on her employer but does not accept the legitimacy of her own sub-ordination in the social order, she is not a deferential worker. The unpaid domestic worker, on the other hand, is dependent on her husband, but usually accepts the legitimacy of her own subordination and is a deferential wife.

Similarly, most of these employers accept the subordinate role of blacks in South African society. Their attitudes towards their domestic servants are only comprehensible in terms of a general racial inferiorisation. The majority, 68 per cent, believed that blacks are generally inferior to whites in their personal qualities; 30 per cent thought they were not inferior and one said she did not know. Some commented:

They haven't the same standards as us.

Yes, they're inferior in every way.

I only know farm natives. They are all stupid and irresponsible. In short, very raw.

The standards of farm natives are so low. They don't seem to want to improve . . . they're most unreliable and they're becoming worse. The old faithfuls are dying out. The younger ones have no respect for any one.

You have to battle to teach them . . . they slide back again after three days.

It's not a fair question . . . they haven't progressed far enough for us to compare.

If they're away from work for two or three weeks they don't worry . . . they have no sense of responsibility.

They are very mentally inferior. They don't think like us . . . you only get the odd one with a bit of intelligence.

They need guidance all the time.

They do such stupid things . . . but I suppose some are coming up quite nicely.

Yes, even the educated ones are different to us.

Yes, they're stupid and irresponsible.

Yes, they've just come out of the trees. (laughs) I mean, they are at a lower stage in the evolutionary ladder.

Blacks have a different attitude to life. They don't believe in hard work.

They are potentially equal, but it will take two to three generations.

A native is a funny thing . . . they're lazy. They don't want to do extra work . . . so they sometimes pretend to be stupid.

They're different . . . they love running around.

On the whole they're stupid . . . raw. They've got no brains.

No, but they need a lot of help. They don't understand about modern life.

They've got a long way to go in evolutionary terms. Putting them in European clothes doesn't make them civilised.

No, but we've got thousands of years of civilisation behind us which blacks haven't got.

It's a stupid question. You can't compare whites and natives. We have centuries of education and decent home living behind us.

They're not inferior but they're not equal to us.

I don't look down on them. They can't help being what they are.

No, they're not inferior but the outside world is causing trouble for us.

Yes, I feel very sorry for them most of the time. They don't have the opportunities in life to better themselves.

They're black and we're white . . . you can't compare us.

They do terrible things but I don't hate blacks . . . they are also God's creatures.

I treat them fairly but I have my reserves. I can't get myself to want to share a table or anything else with them.

No, if only they all kept themselves clean. We can't be expected to sit in a bioscope (cinema) with such smelly people.

Yes, they're irresponsible . . . they don't think of the future . . . Drunkenness among the men is the main trouble. They spend R4000 on drink in this location every weekend. Then the women and children don't get enough to eat. Many women abandon their babies. At least one a month is found in the rubbish bins at Kingswood College. They throw them away because they can't feed them.

Although the majority of these women believe that blacks are inferior to whites in personal qualities, 44 per cent think they are not treated fairly, 48 per cent feel they are treated fairly, and 8 per cent said they did not know. Several expressed their disquiet at discussing this topic:

We're getting into deep water now.

I hope I'm not going to have the Special Branch after me (nervous laughter) but no . . . the list of their grievances is endless.

Others said:

Yes, but they must work for what they get. The more they get the more they sit and wait for it. I don't mind seeing a well-dressed, well-educated native – one who's clean and well behaved.

Yes, I've always treated my servants well. (The equation of blacks and servants in this employer's mind is obvious.)

They're treated fairly.

We must understand that they're different from us. They look at things in a different way.

They should have more say in the running of affairs.

The Group Areas Act is bad. My daughter couldn't take her farm girl up to the Transvaal with her to look after her children.

No, they don't get equal pay for equal work.

They lack political rights.

No, they're not fairly taxed . . . proportionately they pay more than whites.

Yes, take education. Few of them make it to Matric . . . but you have to spend more on Matric than on Standard I pupils.

Yes, their schools look inferior but it's the parents' fault. Their parents don't get behind them and push.

Yes, the government does a lot for the natives.

I don't know how they can complain . . . it's all nonsense.

I don't know.

I've never thought they were treated too badly.

They can't own anything . . . not their houses or any land.

I don't know anyone who treats blacks unfairly.

No, why must they pay for school books?

They're not given sufficient opportunity in any field.

Yes, they're well treated . . . especially compared to other African states.

No, what about job reservation?

No, people treat them like animals.

No, not always. I know I treat mine well but I have heard of people just walking up to a native and slapping or kicking him for no reason.

Yes, but they're getting spoilt . . . they want everything now.

No, not always . . . they are pushed under and not given a fair deal in many ways. They live in hovels . . . but until they lift themselves up we can't love them. There's so much disease and ugliness . . .

Overall, job reservation for whites, low wages, lack of political rights, unfair taxation, inferior education, lack of opportunities generally, poor housing, restrictions on ownership and undignified treatment, were cited as instances of their unfair treatment.

A surprising number (seventeen) had never heard of the Black Consciousness movement. One commented, 'You mean the Black Sash?' This attitude is surprising in view of the fact that during the period in which these interviews took place almost all the leaders of this movement were being detained without trial in Grahamstown prison. There had been several items in the local newspapers about them. None of these women made a positive comment about the Black Consciousness movement. Some were:

> Horrible . . . these people are coming up too fast and expecting too much.

> It's a great pity.

> Inevitable, it had to come . . . there must be more of it percolating than we realise.

Most were reluctant to discuss the topic and were not interested in it. When these women were asked what they felt about the difference in living conditions between blacks and whites generally in South Africa, twenty-four expressed no disquiet. Of these, seventeen specifically expressed no disquiet, four actually felt anxious to see black living conditions improving, and thus the gap between black and white living conditions closing, and three denied the existence of a great difference in living conditions. On the other hand, twenty-six of the employers expressed disquiet and many felt the difference was wrong or sad. A response which appeared in many different forms centred on the notion that 'they have different needs to us':

> They don't think and feel like we do.

> There's a difference but it doesn't hurt them. They are used to it. They wouldn't know what to do with our standards . . . but they're improving all the time. They never used to wear bloomers for instance. A pair of bloomers was not heard of in this district.

> You can't compare natives and us.

> You can't compare town and farm natives. Farm natives wouldn't like to live as we do. They would hate to sit at a table to eat.

> They don't think like we do.

Some comments blamed blacks for their poor living conditions:

They would make pigsties of nice houses.

Many are desperately poor here. But they could impove their own living standards by growing their own vegetables.

They all need bathrooms. (Laughter.)

Those who live in town and earn these fantastic salaries don't live any better. They spend it all on their backs and on liquor.

The trouble is that today natives try to be like white people . . . then they get into debt and are full of complaints. But it's all their own fault.

They don't know how to use their money. My gardener spends all his wages on drink.

The better type natives should improve their living conditions. Others you can't help . . . they will always live in hovels.

They should improve matters themselves. If you're not happy at home how can you be happy at work?

Their over-breeding is the problem.

Their living conditions are very bad. The trouble is they can't save. They spend their money as they get it.

They spend their money badly. They buy flashy furniture and butter rather than margarine.

Other comments were:

Most of them are happy as they are.

Those who are ready for it are moving forward.

I feel a bit sorry for them sometimes.

They shouldn't be held back . . . I would dearly like to see the difference in living conditions narrowed.

It must be terrible for them to be in such a low state.

Education in the younger ones is making them discontented . . . maybe their education is indoctrination.

I've recently come here from Britain and the difference is striking. It makes me very uncomfortable.

It makes me feel sick with guilt.

Sometimes I think we have too much . . . especially when it rains. If they had better housing it would help.

Some natives and coloureds have a better home than I have.

Our locations are bad, but compared to the Far East, their houses are palatial.

It's bad but we can do nothing.

They've got their place and we've got ours . . . the difference in living conditions doesn't really worry me.

There's a great difference but I can see no way of solving this problem.

Some blacks live well . . . better than us even. They have big cars and expensive clothing.

I could be put in jail for saying this, but I'd like to see a more open society where there are fewer controls and restrictions.

Some blacks live in expensive houses.

Bad . . . they should have electricity and tapped water.

I try to push it to the back of my mind.

They're coming close to living like us. They're getting cheeky, they want to wear fancy clothes and they don't take their hats off when they speak to you any more.

Only 16 per cent said they felt strongly about the difference between black and white living conditions. One of these said she would 'commit suicide' if she had to change places with her servant. However, the majority, 68 per cent, said they expect the difference in living conditions between blacks and whites generally in South Africa to change. Expectations as to when this change would come about varied a good deal. Only 6 per cent thought it would come about in their own lifetime, 8 per cent thought it would come about in their children's lifetime, 54 per cent thought that although change was inevitable some time, it was impossible to predict when, and 32 per cent said they did not know or felt confused on this issue. While most of these women, 66 per cent, expressed apprehension about the future, 34 per cent expressed none and nine of these thought no change was likely to occur in the future. Some said:

I'm worried about the future . . . servants make bad masters.

I'm very pessimistic about the future. We've missed the opportunity to have peaceful change. This country could have been utopia . . . violent change is not going to be good for black or white.

I'm an optimist by nature . . . I live each day as it comes.

I'm not afraid for the future, but my husband is. We are on the frontier here . . . he wants me to join the Pistol Club.

I'm scared we'll be ruled by natives.

I'm petrified for my children. I wish the world would leave us alone . . . we're being pushed too fast.

I'm worried about the future . . . we don't know what's going to happen to these people.

Many people are terrified. The cards seem to be stacked against us . . . all this military build up.

Change is inevitable . . . but I'm very apprehensive about the future if it involves black rule. Servants will turn on us.

South Africa will go the same way as Rhodesia.

The natives are getting greedy.

Every woman with children is worried about the future. They're pushing down on us from the North.

I feel confused mainly . . . all through history people have had nasty situations to cope with and they've survived.

I'm worried about the future for my children because of the Bantu problem. The Bantu are not satisfied . . . they want more and more.

I'm afraid for my sons. The government is power crazy. It will push the blacks into revolt.

The present situation can't go on but I try not to think about it too much.

The future will work itself out.

Sometimes I feel desperate. I'm afraid that changes will come too late and that we whites won't be able to live in this country any more.

They're dangerous now . . . the trouble is they're having so many children.

Sometimes I worry . . . in the old days there wasn't the hatred there is today.

I'm apprehensive . . . I would hate to have to work for a black.

We're sitting on a powder keg . . . the whole thing will blow up in our faces.

This last comment illustrates something which struck me very forcibly – that these women are living with fear. The affluence and outward complacency of their lives contrasts very sharply with this deep-seated sense of strain, tension and insecurity. This fear could be illustrated in countless ways. Many homes I visited had elaborate security precautions: burglar bars, security gates, alarm systems and guard dogs. During the period of field work, the crime rate and 'the Bantu problem' were common topics of conversation outside academic circles. In Grahamstown people were warned by the Commandant of Police not to open their doors to people begging for bread. (*Grocott's Daily Mail*, 7.7.1978.) In Port Alfred the local paper advised that children should be instructed in the use of fire-arms. (*The Kowie Announcer*, December 1978.) The purchase of fire-arms has soared since 1976 and many people talk about emigration. In psychological terms South Africa is a 'siege society'. In political terms South Africa is increasingly becoming a 'garrison state', and in this atmosphere black servants may come to be viewed with increasing suspicion.[10]

Mphahlele has focused on this image of 'the menacing servants'. In a penetrating discussion of the white man's image of the 'non-white' in fiction, he shows that in the work of both Nadine Gordimer and Doris Lessing servants are viewed as subtly and ironically menacing. Both writers:

in their image of the African – the servant in particular – bring out clearly this one fact: that the whites in Africa live in fat feudal comfort which the servant class affords them. And even although they do not pay these workers well, the whites lose heavily: their humaneness. A kind of moral corrosion has set in this privileged society. And what is more, they are never sure, by virtue of this master-servant relationship, what goes on in the mind of this seeming black automaton. But it is a menacing automaton. (Mphahlele, 1962: 145.)

This notion of 'menace' is especially relevant to the current South African situation, which is marked by an escalation of resistance, of state repression, and of racial distrust.

7 Struggles

A victory on every page
Who cooked the victory feast?
Berthold Brecht

There can be no freedom of society whilst women are
in bondage.
Women's Charter, 1954

This book has attempted to show that domestic workers are largely 'trapped' workers. As black women they are trapped in a vulnerable and powerless situation within which they are subject to oppression and exploitation.

Their exploitation is evidenced by deprivation of their family life, of reasonable working hours, of time to pursue social and leisure interests of their own choosing, of a negotiated wage, of favourable working conditions, of the ability to rent or purchase accommodation in a chosen place, to sell their labour in the place of their choice, of respectful treatment, of the acknowledgement of the dignity and importance of their labour, of legal protection, of membership in an effective worker organisation, of effective bargaining power, of regular paid leave – all of which show a great deal of variability between different areas and employers, but exist in an extreme form in the Eastern Cape.

In the sample of 225 households investigated in the Eastern Cape, wages ranged from £3.30 to £20 a month. According to the domestic worker informants, full-time workers earned an average (arithmetic mean) wage of £7.58 per month. Almost three-quarters of the sample earned below £10 a month. Payment in kind is generally of a haphazard nature and far lower than it is commonly believed to be. All the domestic workers in the depth sample received some food daily, but the quantity and quality varied widely. Almost half the sample received no meat at all.

No strong positive correlation was found between wages and working hours. Full-time servants worked an average of sixty-one hours per week. The hours ranged from forty to eighty-five hours per week with 77.7 per cent working *more* than a 48-hour week. Almost a third of the total sample work a seven-day week. Eighty-three per cent have to work on public holidays and 23 per cent are given no annual holiday. Only 40 per cent of those who are given an annual holiday are paid during this period.

There is no government legislation stipulating their minimum wages, hours of work, or other conditions of service. Domestic workers thus exist in a legal vacuum. Most are driven into wage labour by the need to support their families. Lack of education opportunities and employment alternatives, coupled with influx control legislation restricting the movement of black workers, all combine to trap black women generally, and in the Eastern Cape most specifically, in domestic service. Domestic workers on farms are in an especially trapped situation as they move only with their specific employer. Thus they constitute a totally tied labour force.

It has been suggested that the key to understanding the domestic workers' situation lies in their powerlessness and dependence on their employers. The employers set wages and conditions of work according to their own preference. These are usually decidedly disadvantageous to the workers. The predominant response obtained from the domestic servants interviewed in the Eastern Cape is a sense of being trapped; of having no viable alternatives; of living out an infinite series of daily frustrations, indignities and denials.

The dependence of domestic servants on their employers is often taken to imply that they are deferential workers. Evidence from this research suggests that the deference attributed to domestic servants is more apparent than real. Many domestic servants adopt a mask of deference as a protective disguise. This enables them to conform to employer expectations and shield their real feelings. Domestic servants are not deferential workers but trapped workers. This is true of black workers in South Africa generally, who are among the most regimented labour forces in the world. Ultimately, then, the problems of domestic servants are generated by a system which does not operate in their interests.

However, African women in South Africa have an impressive history of organised resistance to that system. The best known illustration of this resistance is the anti-pass demonstration by 20,000 women on 9 August 1956. On that day women travelled to Pretoria from all over the country to present thousands of petitions to the Prime Minister, Mr J.G. Strydom, protesting against the extension of passes to African women. After standing in silence for half an hour the women sang the now famous song:

> Now you have touched the women
> you have struck a rock.
> You have dislodged a boulder.
> You will be crushed.

During this period of mass political mobilisation in the 1950s women were involved in various protests in addition to the anti-pass campaign: the Defiance campaign against racist laws; boycotts of beer halls; and protests against Bantu Education. In the rural areas women resisted compulsory cattle dipping, tax increases and land expropriation. In 1954 a national body, the Federation of South African Women (FEDSAW) was formed. It was composed of organised groups of women such as the ANC Women's League. At the inaugural conference a Women's Charter was adopted in which women called for solidarity in the struggle against apartheid racism, sexism and economic exploitation.

For both African men and women the primary struggle has been and remains the struggle against apartheid. Black women are active in the three dominant ideological and organisational currents that challenge apartheid and have support amongst the black majority. These are, first, the non-racial democratic position articulated traditionally by the African National Congress (ANC), and more recently by the United Democratic Front (UDF); second, the racially exclusive Black Consciousness movement; and third, the independent labour movement, particularly the Congress of South African Trade Unions (COSATU). Black women have been at the forefront of the crucial political campaigns of the 1980s; in boycotts, stay-aways, and in grassroots community organisations. African women were the initiators of the consumer boycott of white-owned shops which was launched in 1985 and was one of the most important strategies for change to emerge within South Africa in recent years. This developed into a national consumer boycott with four demands: the lifting of the state of emergency; the removal of the police and the army from the townships; the release of all detainees; and political rights for all South

Africa's people. As African women are responsible for organising household consumption, and in particular for doing the household shopping, it was African women who suffered the inconvenience and often added expense which the boycott of white shops involved. It was these women who had to do more domestic labour in order to stretch the wage further.

Trade unions are another important vehicle through which African women are challenging apartheid. Clearly organisation in trade unions is essential not only for women workers to win maternity rights, better pay and working conditions, but to avoid the unorganised and low paid woman worker being used to undercut the male worker. It is in this sense that the black working class as a whole stands to gain from women being well organised, active trade unionists. As Maggie Magubane says, 'One thing is for sure, if we don't address the problems the bosses will play the women off against the men.' (Barrett *et al.*, 1985: 116.) At present the sexual division of labour divides the working class in South Africa and thus contributes to maintaining its sub-ordination as a whole.

There is a growing movement to organise domestic workers into trade unions as part of this process of challenging apartheid capitalism. Before the 1980s the best known initiatives were those of employers. The Domestic Workers' and Employers' Project (DWEP) was started in 1970 and aimed to support domestic workers and help them to change the conditions of their lives. DWEP founded hundreds of 'Centres of Concern' where domestic workers came together to socialise and to acquire skills. Domestic workers have also taken significant initiatives to organise themselves.

The most important development in recent years was the launch, in November 1986, of a new national union, the South African Domestic Workers Union (SADWU). The union is now 52,000 members strong and is affiliated to COSATU. (See Appendix 3.)

As Florence de Villiers, one of the key movers behind the formation of SADWU acknowledged, domestic workers are notoriously difficult to organise. Unprotected by law, and totally dependent on their employers for shelter and food, they often, in her words, simply 'have no alternative. They are controlled by their employers.' But she had not come across any workers 'who are unwilling to be organised, although there is a lot of fear involved', she said. (*Weekly Mail*, 28.11.1986.) The atomised and scattered nature of the workforce creates considerable difficulties. Margaret Nlapo, general secretary of the Johannesburg branch of SADWU, said that 'thus far recruitment has predominantly been based on word of mouth. We do sometimes send an organiser to a new area, but it is important to know that every member is an organiser for SADWU.' In addition, the lack of time off means that the union has to have 'a follow-up meeting the next day, for those who couldn't come the day before'. (*South African Labour Bulletin*, vol.2, no.2, January 1987, p.48.)

According to Margaret Nlapo, 'domestic workers take a long time to come around . . . Domestic workers are isolated and it is important that they should not feel this isolation. It should be broken down, they should mix with other workers and see themselves as the same as other workers and then they will gain a lot of fighting spirit because they will know the history of other workers' fighting until they got what they wanted. It builds them up, and makes them enthusiastic. They are now getting organised and educated and it helps working-class unity.' (Interview by B. van Rooyen, 1.4.1987.)

According to the President of SADWU, 'the new union will maintain unity in the working-class struggle under the umbrella of COSATU. It will also work with other progressive organisations to fight for a democratic South Africa.' It is thus clear that domestic workers specifically and black women generally are playing an increasingly important role in that struggle.

One of the most impressive cases of black women – including domestic workers – mobilising to demonstrate their unity and strength is the Port Alfred stayaway. When police refused to charge a rapist and detained five schoolgirls, the Port Alfred Women's Organisation (PAWO) decided to organise a week-long stayaway:

> The stayaway was supported by all African working women in the township. Several thousand stayed away from work. Most are domestic workers, and a few employed in factories or shops. (Forrest and Jochelsen, 1986: 25.)

This was described as 'the first stayaway of its kind in South Africa'. (*South African Labour Bulletin*, vol.11, no.6, June 1986, p.53.) The reaction from their employers is illuminating:

> The white community was unsympathetic and just got angry. They doubted our word, questioning why we had not taken action before, if this man was known to have attacked in the past. We think white women were only worried about the work they

now had to do in their own houses. (PAWO member, cited by Forrest and Jochelson, 1986: 26.)

The reaction from white employers was not only unsympathetic but totally uncomprehending:

Throughout the week no black women workers put in an appearance in Port Alfred. White employers, who mostly dealt with their maids under the most benevolent conditions, turning a blind eye to sickness, short hours, inexperienced work and the disappearance of acknowledged 'perks', rolled up their sleeves and got stuck into the housework, saying the maids should band together and confront the intimidators with the facts – that such behaviour as total strikes only led to poverty and starvation, as well as increasing ill-will between the races. (*Grocott's Coastal News*, 13.5.1986.)

Generally, the white community also appears to have interpreted this event in a 'reds under the beds' framework. For example, the local white newspaper reflected:

FOOD FOR THOUGHT

1 Every stayaway, boycott or incident involving large groups of people must be organised and directed by someone.
2 Someone must have given orders for the latest stayaway.
3 The reason for the stayaway must be politically inspired.
(*The Kowie Announcer*, 9.5.1986.)

A member of PAWO, Koleka Nkwinti, was detained and interrogated by the police about the stayaway:

'The police asked me who was behind the stayaway. They couldn't believe women organised it themselves. They detained the male activists, because they think men are behind everything women do,' she said. (Forrest and Jochelson, 1986: 26.)

Such responses are clearly informed by a deep contempt for black women, anchored in both the sexist and racist stereotypes of dependence and inferiority. Such stereotypes are frequently used in South Africa to deny and trivialise women's political commitment. (Cock, 1988.)

In the last few years action to unite South African women in the fight for justice and peace has grown. On 25 April 1987 women from all over South Africa gathered in Cape Town to launch the Women's Congress Alliance. It is hoped that a revived Federation of South African Women (FEDSAW) will unite women who are against apartheid. This initiative is part of a current mobilisation of mass-based opposition organisations that is bearing the full force of the state's repression.

State repression is aimed at eliminating organised resistance in order to restore stability and manage reform. Its strategy involves two broad strands: first to disorganise mass-based opposition through detentions without trial. It is estimated that something of the order of 30,000 people have been detained for lengthy periods since the declaration of the first state of emergency in 1986. This number includes numerous women such as Sister Bernard Ncube, the President of the Federation of Transvaal Women (FEDTRAW), who spent over a year in detention. At the time of writing (August 1988) a FEDSAW organiser, Joyce Mashomba, has been detained without trial since August 1986. The second strand in the current state strategy of repression involves closing off the legal space within which anti-apartheid groupings have operated. The banning of meetings, press curbs, restrictions on certain organisations and individuals, the regulations controlling funerals and prohibiting calls for boycotts and strikes are part of this process of closure.

At the time of writing there is a widespread sense of defeat and demoralisation over non-violent struggles against apartheid. The state of emergency has lasted for over three years and women's organisations are struggling to survive. However, the importance of our struggle is recognised by increasing numbers of people all over the world. These people are coming to recognise that the South African apartheid system 'is perhaps uniquely vicious in its degree of exploitation and repression'. (Davies, 1973: 56.)

This book has attempted to document one particular aspect of that exploitation. At the same time I have tried to emphasise the extraordinary strengths and competences black women have developed within this oppressive structure and which bear witness to their power to endure, to survive and nurture life amidst the violence and social disintegration of contemporary South Africa. As Angela Davis has written of black women in America: 'Black women could hardly strive for weakness: they had to become strong for their families and their communities needed their strength to survive.' (Davis, 1982: 231.) Davis identifies one of the greatest ironies of the slave system in the

USA as the process of 'subjecting women to the most ruthless exploitation conceivable' which at the same time strengthened their capacity to resist.

The same contradictory process is at work in contemporary South Africa. Their strengths should inspire all people's struggle for equality and freedom everywhere.

Notes and References

Chapter 2

1 Quoted in Francis Wilson and Dominique Perrot, eds, *Outlook on a Century, 1870–1970* (Lovedale, Press, SPROCAS, Lovedale, 1973), p.563.
2 I have converted wages to pounds sterling at the rate of exchange prevailing at the time the book was being researched: approximately 3 rand to the pound.
3

Age Range of a Sample of 50 Domestic Workers

Age range	Number	Percentage
15–19	0	
20–24	0	
25–29	3	6
30–34	1	2
35–39	11	22
40–44	9	18
45–49	17	34
50–54	3	6
55–59	2	4
60–64	3	6
65–69	1	2

4 In terms of the Bantu Taxation Act, employers have to register their domestic workers and pay a tax on any Bantu whose wage exceeds R30 (£10) a month. On a monthly wage of R30 to R40 a tax of 10 cents is payable. Tax payable on monthly wages in excess of R40 increases on a sliding scale. The employer is meant to deduct this tax from the wages of the employee and is liable to a fine or to imprisonment or to both for not doing so.
5 Mayer, 1979:18. From 1974 there was a change in the influx control regulations so that for the purposes of labour movement the Cape Midlands region is now seen as one unit.
6 There are many echoes here of Miss Matty's 'Martha' in Elizabeth Gaskell's *Cranford*.

7 'Servant's meat' refers to the cheapest cuts of meat available, such as chuck and brisket.

8 This temptation is beautifully described by Bennett in Elsie's response to some leftover steak. 'The steak during its cooking, had caused her a lot of inconvenience; the smell of it had awakened desires which she had had difficulty in withstanding; it had made her mouth water abundantly; and she had been very thankful to get the steak safely into the dining room without any accident happening to it.' Elsie wrestles with temptation, succumbs, eats the steak and then suffers agonies of remorse, as she did whenever she pilfered food.

9 'Southern folklore abounds with charming stories of slaves outwitting masters by behaving like black versions of the Good Soldier Schweik. The trouble is that too often the masters enjoyed being out-witted in the same way that a tyrannical father sometimes enjoys being out-witted by a child. Every contortion necessary to the job implied inferiority. It proved the slave a clever fellow; it hardly proved him a man. It gained a few privileges or crumbs but undermined self-respect and confirmed the master's sense of superiority. The post-slavery tradition of obsequiousness, indirection and the wearing of a mask before white men has played a similar role in the south ever since.' (Eugene Genovese, 'The Legacy of Slavery and Roots of Black Nationalism', in James Weinstein and David Eakins, eds, *For a New America* (Vintage Books, New York, 1970), p.400.)

10 Antrobus states that in the Eastern Cape (defined to include a much larger area than in this study), 'some farm labourers are allowed free grazing rights'. (G. Antrobus, 'Farm Labour in the Eastern Cape 1950–1973'. Unpublished paper. August, 1976, p.7.) Only one of the small sample of farms investigated in this study allowed this.

11 Cash wages paid throughout the Eastern Cape are low. Antrobus (in Wilson *et al.*, 1977:12) found the monthly cash wage paid on 299 farms in the Eastern Cape in 1973 to be an average R10.67 (about £3.55) with a median of R9.89. He reports that 15 per cent of the farmers surveyed were paying permanent workers a cash wage of R5 or less per month; 45 per cent were paying between R6 and R10; 20 per cent between R11 and R15; and a further 20 per cent between R16 and R30. He estimates the monthly cash wage to constitute only about one fifth to one quarter of total remune-ration, with rations making up another quarter. Thus domestic

workers on farms are in a special position of exploitability and exploitation.

Overall, farm workers are an exploited group: 'They are among the lowest paid in the South African economy: denied access to elementary political rights or to collective bargaining processes, and unprotected by statutory minimum wage legislations. Black farm workers are also prevented by lack of schooling, lack of skills and an apparently chronic shortage of urban housing from seeking alternative industrial employment. African workers are, in addition, trapped on the farms by legislation restricting their movements.'

12 Quoted in the *Eastern Province Herald*, 24.9.1979.

13 Quoted ibid., 7.11.1978.

14 Since 1978 wages have increased so that in 1986 the average month's cash wage for full-time domestic workers in South Africa was £11.30 ('Central Statistical Service survey, reported in the *Weekly Mail*, 5.2.1988). However, the increase should be set against an inflation rate that has been 18 per cent per annum for some years now.

15 Clarke, who carried out a study of domestic servants in Salisbury, found that the average domestic servant worked 63.5 hours a week. None worked less than eight hours daily, and some as many as eighteen hours. (D. Clarke, *Domestic Workers in Rhodesia* (Mambo Press, Gwelo, 1974), p.36.) In a Fort Victoria study Weinrich found that 70 per cent worked between nine and thirteen hours a day and 12 per cent worked longer than fourteen hours a day. The writer comments, 'Such long working days are unknown in the industry and this is another reason why most Africans prefer any employment to domestic work.' (Weinrich, 1976: 238.) In her Cape Town study of domestic workers Spektor found that weekly working hours averaged sixty-one. (Spektor, 1977.) Mrs Leah Tutu of DWEP is quoted as saying, 'Our experience is that most domestics work a 12-hour day during the week.' (Quoted in the *Eastern Province Herald*, 28.11.1978.)

16 P. Horn, *The Rise and Fall of the Victorian Servant* (Gill & Macmillan, Dublin, 1975), pp.50–51. Burnett suggests that 'eighty hours of work a week, against fifty-six for the factory worker, may well be a fair estimate for the late nineteenth century [in Britain] and must have been exceeded in many single-handed households'. (Burnett, 1977: 171.)

17 See 'My Night as a Squatter', by Brendon Roberts, in *South African Outlook*, March 1977, for a moving description of the housing conditions of squatters.

18 See 'Housing Conditions for Migrant Workers in Cape Town', *Financial Mail*, 7.1.1977.

Chapter 3

1 Prostitution was not mentioned at all by respondents. According to Willsworth, there are only twenty-five prostitutes in Grahamstown's black community. (Willsworth, 1979: 108.) This is surprising. In nineteeth-century Britain, domestic servants were one of the major sources of prostitution. As Davidoff comments, 'that the loneliness and privations of the life of a woman in a small household might make even prostitution look attractive, was never considered'. (L. Davidoff *et al.*, 'Landscape with Figures: Home and Community in English Society', pp.139–75 in J. Mitchell and A. Oakley eds, *The Rights and Wrongs of Women* (Penguin, Harmondsworth, 1976), p.168.) Weinrich found that many prostitutes had been domestic servants – in the past. (Weinrich, 1973:109.) The very position of domestic servants – low wages, poor accommodation, no possibilities of promotion – helps to project these underprivileged women into prostitution. A link between the two occupational categories seems plausible, but would need to be tested by further research.

2 This contrasts with 34.9 per cent of their white employers.

3 Iona Mayer, 'Grahamstown'. Unpublished research project, 1979, p.104.

4 About half the domestic workers in both Walther's Johannesburg study and Whisson and Weil's Cape Town study 'lived in'.

5 How to address servants is a common theme in British nineteenth-century handbooks on etiquette and household management. Burnett quotes a writer who thought that 'It is better in addressing servants to use a higher key of voice, and not to suffer it to fall at the end of a sentence.' (Burnett, 1977: 173.)

6 Of course, many of the characteristics of total institutions also apply to the compounds of migrant workers in South Africa.

7 Resentment against the employer's dogs is a theme in Ezekiel Mphahlele's short story, 'Mrs Plum'. (E. Mphahlele, *In Corner B* (East Africa Publishing House, Nairobi, 1967), p.177.)

8 This is contrary to what I had expected. 'Lonely occupations, such as domestic service and lodging house keeping, have high suicide rates.' (Parker *et al.*, *The Sociology of Industry* (George Allen & Unwin, London, 1967), p.144.) In his study of domestic service in

the United States of America between 1870 and 1920, Katzman reports that 'loneliness was a frequent complaint of domestics'. (D. Katzman, *Seven Days A Week. Women and Domestic Service in Industrializing America* (Oxford University Press, New York, 1978), p.14.)

9 Irritation provoked by close supervision is a frequent theme in studies of domestic work generally. For example, 'That really gets me, somebody showing me how to clean.' (Maggie Holmes in Studs Terkel, *Working* (Penguin, Harmondsworth, 1977), pp.112–18.)

10 Van der Vliet and Bromberger report that some farmers in the Eastern Cape find that domestic help is sometimes more difficult to obtain than seasonal help. They suggest 'this may be connected with the fact that domestic work is often individual (rather than done in a group), subject to close supervision and the vagaries of employer personality, often demeaning in terms of skills, and perhaps involves longer hours in the evenings or over weekends'. (Wilson *et al.*, 1977:125.)

11 Domestic service accepted entrants at an early age, 'typically at twelve or thirteen in the mid-nineteenth century – without previous experience or training; it offered them the opportunity of learning those skills associated with homemaking which, hopefully, they would be able to employ in later married life; it provided board and lodging as well as a cash wage, in a sheltered environment where a young girl or boy would be subject to the control and moral care of older servants and employers. In this sense employment in a good household was akin to membership of an extended family group. It was a secure and regular occupation, for which there was a steady demand both in town and country, and for the ambitious it provided a clearly defined route to respected and responsible positions. Above all it reduced the strain on a poor family's budget and living accommodation by removing daughters from over-crowded households as soon as they were old enough to be of use to another.' (Burnett, 1977:137.)

12 For example, John Ruskin, who 'washed a flight of stone stairs all down with bucket and broom, in a Savoy inn, where they hadn't washed their stairs since they first went up them; and I never made a better sketch than that afternoon'. (Ruskin, *Sesame and Lilies* (George Allen & Unwin, London, 1808), p.199.)

13 P. Mayer, 1961:245. 'Red people' are 'the traditionalist Xhosa, the conservatives who still stand by the indigenous way of life,

including the pagan Xhosa religion'. 'School people' are 'products of the mission and the school, holding up Christianity, literacy and other Western ways as ideals'. (Mayer, 1961:4.)

14 In 1979 the R10.50 a week wage 'floor' below which workers may not contribute to or receive benefits from the Unemployment Insurance Fund, would operate to exclude many domestic workers anyway. The Unemployment Insurance Amendment Bill scrapped this wage 'floor', but agricultural and domestic workers are still excluded from the Fund, irrespective of what they earn. (*Financial Mail*, 16.2.1979.)

15 Burnett 1977:169. In America between 1870 and 1920 Katzman maintains that 'the problem of atomisation was truly insurmountable'. (Katzman, 1978:235.)

16 Quoted in Georgina Hill, *Women in English Life from Medieval to Modern Times* (Bentley, London, 1869), 2 vols, p. 221.

Chapter 4

1 Mary Wollstonecraft, quoted by C. Tomalin, *The Life and Death of Mary Wollstonecraft* (Penguin Books, Harmondsworth, 1977), p.105. While Wollstonecraft was writing and involved in the London intellectual scene in the 1780s, her maid took care of the domestic chores. 'In 1788 she . . . was dependent on her maid for the basic organisation of her life, the sweeping, washing and fire-lighting; probably she fetched what food was needed too.' She was 'a necessary fixture who remained in the shadows and was never named in any letters . . .' (Tomalin, 1977:105.) It would be interesting to know how many eminent women have employed other women to do their domestic work. Certainly this applied to even some radical women such as Colette and Kathie Kollwitz.

2 In the Eastern Cape black people are termed 'Kafs', 'Afs', 'wogs', 'coons', 'kaffirs', 'munts', 'natives', and 'Bantu', as well as the less derogatory terms of blacks and Africans. In the rural areas black people are sometimes termed 'Wilbies'. The most plausible explanation of this extraordinary nomenclature that has been suggested to me is that they were championed by Wilberforce in the last century. This explanation brings the slave analogy to the forefront.

3 The importance of knowing their African first name is illustrated in Mphahlele's short story 'Mrs Plum'.

4 For instance, in Papua, New Guinea, early this century. (See Inglis, 1975:21-2.)

Chapter 5

1 For this chapter I found Newby's insightful analysis of agricultural workers extremely suggestive. (See especially Chapter 7, in Newby, 1977.)
2 Newby makes this point about agricultural workers in Britain. (Newby, 1977:387.)

Chapter 6

1 The following incident may convey something of the atmosphere of the area. I remember seeing a film called *North West Frontier* in Grahamstown some years ago. When one of the actors stated 'Half the world is only civilised because the British made them so', there was prolonged applause from the audience.
2 Willsworth, 1979:16. Calculated from Table A4 of the 1970 Census.
3 'Rawness' was a frequently mentioned attribute. It is commonly used in the Eastern Cape to indicate the low level of incorporation of a black into 'white culture'.
4 This woman echoes the feelings of George Eliot's Mr Tomlinson in *Scenes of Clerical Life*: 'Give me a servant as can nayther read nor write, I say, and doesn't know the year o' the Lord as she was born in.'
5 Memmi points to the significance of the trait of 'laziness' in the stereotypical conception of the 'colonised'. It is commonly used as a rationalisation for the payment of low wages and inequality in colonial societies. 'Nothing could better justify the coloniser's privileged position than his industry, and nothing could better justify the colonised destitution than his indolence. The mythical portrait of the colonised therefore includes an unbelievable laziness and that of the coloniser a virtuous taste for action. At the same time the coloniser suggests that employing the colonised is not very profitable, thereby authorising his unreasonable wages.' (Memmi, 1974:79.)
6 Only nine employed two domestic servants; one employed three; and one employed four.
7 For this reason the domestic workers' answers were given

separately in Chapter 3, while the employers' are given here.

8 See above, p.34, for the domestic workers' answers to this question.

9 Beechey points to some similarities between the position of married women and semi-proletarianised workers from the point of view of capital. (Beechey, 1977:45–61.)

10 A garrison state is one in which the institutions and the agents who hold military, economic and political power have become closely interdependent, and the boundaries between military and civilian spheres are increasingly loose and amorphous. The movement towards a garrison state is evidenced by, for example, a defence budget which increased to approximately £326 million in 1977; an increasing call-up for military duty (nearly 60,000 civilians in 1977); the increasing militarisation of schools through cadet corps; increasing interest in civil defence – there are now 692 civil defence organisations; the increase in Defence Bond sales; increased sales of war-games and war-toys; and so on.

Appendix I

G'Town Dynamite Attack – Lights out Mystery

Street lights in Cross Street, Grahamstown, went out mysteriously just before a 20 centimetre-long pack of dynamite sticks was hurled through a front window of the home of Rhodes University lecturer, Ms Jacklyn Cock, on Thursday night.

The dynamite landed in the dining room, where she was having a late supper with two friends. It failed to explode but smouldered for about half an hour while police explosives experts worked at removing it.

Lights in Batholomew and Bathurst streets, where they intersect with Cross Street, were also out at 11.30 p.m., when the dynamite was thrown, but the city's Electrical Engineer, Mr G. R. Beard, said he knew of no street light failure in Grahamstown on Thursday night.

Captain A. Oosthuizen, Grahamstown Branch Commander of the Security Police, who is heading the investigation, confirmed yesterday that he was looking into the question of the absent street lights.

An explosives expert who came from Port Elizabeth on Thursday night completed his examination of the explosive yesterday morning and destroyed it, according to Colonel Gerrit Erasmus, Chief of the Security Police in Eastern Cape.

Immediately after the incident five road blocks were erected by police on roads out of Grahamstown but by yesterday police had made no arrests.

Meanwhile, a shaken Ms Cock, 39, left yesterday afternoon for a holiday in Johannesburg, after making a full statement to police.

She is the author of the controversial book on domestic servants, entitled 'Maids and Madams', and is also well-known for her strong feminist views.

Mr Richard de Villiers, a fellow lecturer in the Sociology Department, who was with Ms Cock in the dining room when the incident occurred, described the explosive as three sticks of dynamite bound together with white masking tape and with a single lit fuse.

He estimated that the sticks were each 20 centimetres long and $2\frac{1}{2}$ centimetres in diameter.

'We were eating sandwiches after returning from an evening out when we heard a crash at the window. The dynamite pack rolled over the floor, under the drawn curtain and I immediately shouted for everyone to get out.'

Ms Cock and another friend, Mrs Ingrid Stewart, sought refuge in a bedroom at the back of the house while Mr de Villiers telephoned the police.

'I went outside but saw no-one. We all waited outside for the police, who arrived within minutes of my call.'

Mr de Villiers then accompanied a policeman into the house.

'The dining room was full of smoke but we shone a torch and could see the explosive smouldering. The policeman shouted that it was huge and rushed us all down the street, using his walkie-talkie to summon other policemen.'

Within five minutes the street was swarming with police vehicles and two fire engines stood by as an explosives expert worked on removing the dynamite.

Police vans blocked access to Cross Street at both the Batholomew and Bathurst street corners and evacuated surprised and sleepy residents from neighbouring houses.

Yesterday morning, the place where the explosive had fallen was clearly visible, with a 10 centimetre-long burn on the floorboard. A long scorched streak on the back of the curtain lining indicated where the fuse had dragged down the curtain after it was thrown through the window.

Mr de Villiers said he believed the reason the dynamite had not exploded was because the fuse had been bent or damaged by the curtain and had stopped burning before it could ignite the explosive.

'But it is abundantly clear that someone wanted to kill Jackie. We could have all been blown to smithereens.'

Ms Cock said yesterday that soon after her book 'Maids and Madams' was published last May she started receiving threatening and abusive phone calls.

Sometimes a male voice would threaten her but more often she heard only noises – including the ticking of a clock, ringing of an alarm bell or what sounded like an electronic scream.

After returning to Grahamstown from a two-month recuperation from encephalitis, the calls became more frequent and in the last few weeks they had increased to about five a day.

A few weeks ago she was told: 'You have been sick and we will make you sicker.'

'I didn't report the calls at the time because I did not want to attract attention to myself,' she said.

Eastern Province Herald, 27.12.1980.

Appendix II
Area of Investigation and
Research Procedure

I intended the geographical area of the study to approximate that of the Zuurveld, the area of the Eastern Cape in which the British settlers of 1820 were chiefly located. The area chosen was that covered by the Albany and Bathurst Divisional Councils. This forms a kind of triangle, the apex of which is Grahamstown, the sides of which are the Fish and Bushman rivers, and the base the sea. This is essentially colonial country. It was the cockpit of four frontier wars, and a frontier area socially, culturally, economically and militarily.

The choice of this area ensured that representatives of both rural and urban areas were included. In the rural areas there is a wide variety of agricultural undertakings, with beef and dairy cattle, pineapples, chicory, citrus and mixed farming being the chief activities. The area includes two urban centres. Grahamstown, *Irhini* in Xhosa, is an educational centre. It has a population of over 35,000 Xhosa-speaking people, along with 7000 'coloureds' and 11,000 whites. Port Alfred is a holiday resort with only a fishing industry, a small white community of 2000, and almost 9000 blacks.

Both are non-industrial towns and are sometimes said to be unique in their large black populations and lack of employment opportunities. However, Nyquist shows that Grahamstown is quite typical of smaller cities when evaluated as part of a sample of sixteen small cities from a total thirty-two with populations between 15,000 and 49,000 scattered throughout the four provinces of South Africa. (Nyquist, 1969–70: 23–8.) Further, as the historian W. Macmillan wrote of Grahamstown many years ago:

... from all I can learn of wages and conditions elsewhere I believe it is easy to exaggerate the difference between this and any

country town, and make this an excuse for regarding our own
case as peculiarly insoluble. (Macmillan, 1915: 7.)

Sixty years later his words are still peculiarly apt. Both the urban
centres in the study seem to be quite typical of South Africa's smaller
cities and coastal resorts.

The research techniques were deliberately varied and combined
several methods:

(1) A search of historical sources. Here I was fortunate to have
access to old diaries, newspapers, letters, housekeeping account books
and other family papers which are stored in the Cory Library for
Historical Research, Rhodes Universtiy; (2) participant observation in
the home-work setting; (3) the routine perusal of statistics and the
available literature on domestic workers; (4) a random sample survey,
which was the most important source of data. This involved 225
interviews with domestic workers and employers using interview
schedules.

The interviews attempted to combine the richness of case studies
with the comparability of survey interviews. (Selditz *et al.*, 1959:
235–79.) The most appropriate research instrument appeared to be the
semi-structured interview questionnaire. This technique allows for a
level of spontaneity while ensuring a high degree of comparability
between one interview and another. The framing of questions was
standardised and thus the same substantive material was covered in all
the interviews in order to produce quantifiable data.

The questions were first framed in terms of five informal interviews
with key informants in the community. These were women with an
extensive knowledge of the community and the general situation of
domestic workers. A draft was then prepared and discussed with some
colleagues and friends. On the basis of their criticisms an amended
draft was then tested in the field in a pilot study.

The pilot survey consisted of fifteen interviews conducted during
July 1978. The purpose of the pilot survey was mainly to test the
suitability of the questions on the respondents. On the basis of these
sources of preliminary information, the final interview schedules were
constructed.

Three different interview schedules were used: (i) 125 domestic
workers were briefly interviewed by me using a structured interview
schedule focusing on objective aspects of their work situation; (ii) fifty
domestic workers were interviewed in depth by a field worker using a
semi-structured interview schedule which focused on both objective

and subjective aspects of their situation; (iii) fifty employers of domestic servants were interviewed in depth by me using a semi-structured interview schedule which similarly focused on both objective and subjective aspects.

Interview schedules (ii) and (iii) combined open-ended and fixed choice questions. It was surmised that many of the respondents would not have clearly formulated opinions on many of the issues. To avoid a forced statement of opinion and elicit a free response it was decided to keep some of the questions open-ended. The questions followed a psychological rather than a logical sequence. 'Touchy' questions were placed towards the end of the interview schedule. (Goode and Hatt, 1957: 195.) As Madge writes, 'the principal application of the interview in social science is its use for the purpose of making people talk about themselves'. (Madge, 1965: 150.) The interviewer insisted on complete privacy with the respondent, where this was practicable, in order to encourage an atmosphere in which candour was possible. In the interviews with employers some excluded their husbands reluctantly, while others seemed to enjoy doing so – 'this is woman's talk'. The task of the interviewer was to encourage the respondent to talk freely and fully in response to the questions included in the interview schedule and to make a verbatim record of her replies. This was done with the use of a tape-recorder or shorthand notes.

Experience in the pilot study revealed that a considerable degree of rapport was necessary for a satisfactory interview on the subjects covered, especially those which involved attitudes and emotions. This rapport was established in most cases largely because both interviewers are themselves part of the culture they were exploring. The fifty domestic workers who were studied in depth were interviewed by my field worker, who is a black, Xhosa-speaking woman, from this area, with little formal education, and herself a part-time domestic worker. She was chosen because of these attributes. It was felt that a more educated person might have inhibited the respondents. Her personal qualities of warmth and compassion went a long way to establish trust in her respondents. Indeed, the insights she has elicited on extremely delicate and thorny topics is the most effective tribute to her skill in the interview situation.

Similarly the writer is part of the cultural world of the employers interviewed. I am white, middle-class, of 1820 Settler descent and have lived most of my life in the Eastern Cape. These attributes contributed to overcoming initial suspicion. It is doubtful whether an 'outsider' would have achieved the same results. In addtion some time was spent at the beginning of each interview establishing rapport by exchanging small pieces of conversational information. Certain questions were included in the interview schedule specifically to reinforce such rapport; for example, asking the employers to name the two television programmes they enjoyed the most. This usually elicited some discussion. I followed Beatrice Webb's maxim, 'accept what is offered', and tried not to rush away after the interview session. I often stayed for tea, to chat, look through photographs and scrap books, see over the garden and so on. The depth interviews lasted two hours on average.

The interview schedules were carefully coded, and each question checked for accuracy and reliability before tabulation of the results.

At many points in the field work I felt that this was a study in guilt and fear. The fear was expressed largely by the domestic workers. Several refused to be interviewed at work without their employers' permission, and others were reluctant to be interviewed at all for fear of repercussions from their employers. The guilt was expressed in the response of several employers.

During the pilot survey I introduced myself by saying I was investigating the situation of domestic servants. This provoked a 25 per cent refusal rate. The refusals varied from hostility – 'Haven't you anything better to do?' 'Whatever next . . . No, I'm too busy' – to employers who denied that they employed servants at all. In several cases these women avoided my eye, and were unwilling to open their doors very far. I had the impression the they were lying, and were simply unwilling to be interviewed. One woman said proudly that she did not employ servants because she preferred to be self-reliant and do her own work. It was subsequently reported to me that this woman 'could not keep a servant'. She had employed a series of servants who left because she 'was always chasing after them', and at the time she was approached was employing a servant she had engaged two months previously. On the basis of employers' responses in the pilot survey I changed my method of introduction and said I was doing a study 'on the position of women and the organisation of the home'. This introduction proved far more successful and in the survey proper only three employers refused to be interviewed.

The largest source of difficulty in the study came in arranging interviews with workers without their employers' knowledge. The importance of this was underlined in the pilot study where one domestic reported to the field worker that her employer had subjected her to abuse: 'She shouted at me for telling your madam what I earn. She said I should have said it's none of her business.'

I was aware of the difficulties experienced by previous researchers on other 'delicate' topics in the Eastern Cape. For example, in her study of farm labour, Roberts found that 'the large majority of farmers were not prepared to co-operate with any attempt to interview their labour on conditions of work and work preferences'. (Roberts, 1959: 5.) Studies of domestic workers in other areas reported similar difficulties. For instance, in her study of domestic workers in a Rhodesian community, Weinrich reported that some employers looked on her research with disfavour. 'They feared that if servants were asked questions, they would begin to think of themselves as important people and become insubordinate'. (Weinrich, 1976: 216.) Similarly, in her Durban study, Preston-Whyte reported that 'lack of understanding, suspicion and mistrust of the motives of the study were rife' and many employers were uncooperative. (Preston-Whyte, 1969: 14.) For these reasons, while the initial contact was made by the researcher at the servant's place of work, all the depth interviews took place at the servant's home. These were often extremely difficult to arrange because many of them had little free time.

A further source of difficulty lay in discrepancies in information given. I expected a discrepancy between information given by employers and that given by their workers. This was reported by Roberts who found that 'on a number of farms the picture painted by workers of their conditions of work was certainly less rosy than that conveyed by their employers'. (Roberts, 1959: 5-6.) For this reason the workers' and employers' responses were calculated separately. The employers' accounts of the wages and working hours of their workers did differ from those of the workers themselves.

The domestic workers and employers were interviewed between August 1978 and February 1979. The historical research was started in July 1976. The universe of the study consisted of white households in the Divisional Council of Albany and Bathurst. The areas and populations covered are as follows:

TABLE 1 *Albany Divisional Council Area, 1976*

Population	European	'Coloured' Asiatic	Bantu	Total
Rural	1 803	1 301	28 240	31 344
Urban	14 080	5 511	33 101	52 692

TABLE 2 *Bathurst Divisional Council Area, 1976*

Population	European	'Coloured' Asiatic	Bantu	Total
Rural	1 859	145	23 149	25 153
Urban	2 974	1 025	7 613	11 612

The number of households in the area was computed by dividing the total population by the average household size. According to the 1970 census there are 3.7 persons per household for the white population of South Africa. This gave a total of 487.3 white households in rural Albany, 3,805.4 white households in urban Albany, 502.4 white households in rural Bathurst and 803.8 white households in urban Bathurst.

The distribution of the population in the area thus involved the following population proportions in the sample of 225 households:

TABLE 3 *Sample Proportions*

Area	Short domestic servant interview schedule	Depth domestic servant interview schedule	Depth employer interview schedule
Rural Albany	9	3	3
Urban Albany	85	35	35
Rural Bathurst	12	5	5
Urban Bathurst	19	7	7
Total	125	50	50

The study involved the use of a random multi-stage stratified systematic sample from lists.

The samples were drawn from four sample frames. (i) White household electricity accounts in Grahamstown. This involved drawing 155 addresses from over 3000. Every 22nd address was taken. This constituted the urban Albany sample. (ii) White household electricty accounts in Port Alfred. This involved drawing 33 addresses from almost 800. Every 24th address was taken. This constituted the urban Bathurst sample. (iii) Veterinary Services list of farmers in the Albany district. This involved drawing 15 addresses from 528 farms and smallholdings. Every 35th address was taken. This constituted the rural Albany sample. (iv) Veterinary Services list of farmers in the Bathurst district. This involved drawing 22 addresses from 360 farms and smallholdings. Every 16th address was taken. This constituted the rural Bathurst sample.

A reserve list of the same number for each stratum was made, by listing the preceding address, in case I was unable to make contact with the employer at the original address.

These sampling frames were chosen because they were taken to be the most inclusive of the universe under investigation. The most obvious sampling frame to use, and certainly an easier one, would have been the numbers of registered domestic workers in European households in the area. However this would have excluded the unregistered workers who, it was suspected, constitute a large number, especially in Grahamstown. This was not tested in the study because it could have been used to serve the interests of the officials who administer the influx control regulations. This problem highlights the considerable dangers in social science research. As Nicolaus warns, 'Sociologists stand guard in the garrison and report to its masters on the movement of the occupied populace. The more adventurous sociologists don the disguise of the people and go out to mix with the peasants in the "field", returning with books and articles that break the protective secrecy in which a subjugated population wraps itself, and make it more accessible to manipulation and control.' (Nicolaus, 1972: 39.) This is not the aim of my study.

A sample of 175 domestic servants and fifty employers is undoubtedly small. Are generalisations from the sample population warranted? There is a widespread tendency in social science to assume that a large sample provides some guarantee of reliable results, while a small one suggests unreliability. This is a misconception which:

> is based on a naive idea of what constitutes 'validity' and 'reliability' in research procedure. Statistical representativeness is not, of course, assured simply by means of large numbers; a large sample running into several hundreds or thousands may be selected in a way which makes it unrepresentative of the general population, while a small sample may conversely meet more precisely the criterion of representativeness. (Oakley, 1974: 31.)

Oakley stresses that 'every research study needs to be assessed on the criterion of whether it measures up to its own stated objectives'. (Oakley, 1974: 33.) She writes:

> For the goals of mapping out an area, describing a field and connecting events, processes or characteristics which appear to go together, a sample of forty individuals is certainly adequate. This

kind of taxonomic approach may, perfectly appropriately, give rise to explanatory hypotheses, and particular, well-defined hypotheses may also be tested with samples of this size. In *Theory and Methods of Social Research* Johan Galtung makes a useful distinction between a 'substantive' hypothesis 'which is about social reality and to be tested by means of the data', and a 'generalisation' hypothesis 'which is about the data'. The question as to whether a specific hypothesis is confirmed or not confirmed by the data is in principle different from the issue of whether the research findings can be generalised to a wider population. For testing substantive hypotheses Galtung considers a sample of forty perfectly acceptable (the criterion being the minimum number of cases required for statistical tests to be applicable). On the other hand, to be on the safe side for the purposes of generalisation, a sample size of around eight hundred individuals is needed. (Oakley, 1974: 33.)

Oakley points out that important contributions to sociological knowledge have been made using data from small samples. For instance Bott's influential study *Family and Social Network*, is based on interviews with twenty couples; Hannah Gavron's *The Captive Wife* is based on ninety-six interviews; and Oakley's own study is based on only forty London housewives. This study sets out to describe and explain a situation of exploitation. In the analysis of the data, the conclusions drawn about domestic workers in the Eastern Cape do, strictly speaking, apply only to the research sample. However, as Oakley stresses in her own study, there is no reason to believe that the sample is unrepresentative.

Moser identifies three sources of bias in sample selection: the use of a sampling frame which does not cover the population accurately; the use of a 'non-random' method of sampling so that the selection of subjects is consciously or unconsciously affected by human judgement; and the refusal to cooperate among segments of the chosen population. (Moser, 1958: 73.) In terms of these criteria there is no evidence that the sample is unrepresentative of the wider population in any way.

There are also questions of the researcher's responsibility involved here. 'The researcher who cautiously confines his conclusions to those strictly justified by the data may be safe from criticism, but he is not making his own full potential contribution.' Oakley goes on to say:

It would be shirking one's responsibility not to speculate on how one's own findings may or may not be generalisable beyond the research universe. Important connections to draw are those between one's own findings and the conclusions of other, related research. These are broadly the approaches I adopt. I also operate with the assumption that, although my results pertain strictly only to the sample of forty housewives I interviewed, there is no reason why they should not relate to the wider population of housewives since it cannot be shown that the 40 women are unrepresentative of the larger population. (Oakley, 1974: 35–6.)

This study adopts the same approach. No pretentious claims are made to portray the situation of the 'typical' domestic servant. However, there is no reason to suppose that the fifty employers and 175 domestic servants interviewed are unrepresentative of the larger population. In spite of the small size of the sample the results are probably representative of the area under investigation. Thus while the results pertain strictly to that sample, evidence from other studies and sources is used to argue that domestic servants are an ultra-exploited group of workers, and that their ultra-exploitability derives from the constraints operating on blacks and women generally in South Africa.

Appendix III

South African Domestic Workers' Union:

Resolutions Adopted at the General Conference held at the University of Western Cape on Saturday 29 November 1986

1 Politcal Policy

(a) We believe that the main cause of all violence in South Africa is the existence of the apartheid system, and that there can be no peace while it exists.

So we call:
   (i) For the immediate lifting of the State of Emergency.
   (ii) For the withdrawal of SADF and all apartheid security forces from our townships.
   (iii) For the release of all political prisoners unconditionally and unbanning of banned individuals and organisations.
   (iv) The return of all exiles.

(b) Domestic workers and women should play a major role in the struggle for non-racialism and a democratic society and this organisation will not hesitate to take up political action and to protect and advance the interests of members and the broader struggle. This organisation should do this by taking up political struggles in alliance with other progressive forces of our country that will be done through the membership and structures at local level, regional level and nationally and by affiliating to other political organisations which share the same aim and direction which we envisage to.

2 Working Conditions

Domestic workers are in isolation, therefore we demand:

(i) Minimum wage of R200 per month (£60.70).
(ii) Unemployment Insurance Fund.
(iii) Normal working hours – eight hours a day, five days a week.
(iv) Workmen's Compensation.
(v) Maternity leave.
(vi) Annual leave with full payment.
(vii) Sick leave.
(viii) Overtime at R2.50 per hour (£0.84).

3 Discrimination

(a) Women workers experience both exploitation as workers and oppression as women and black women are further discriminated against on the basis of race.

(b) Women are employed in a limited range of occupations doing boring and repetitive work with low and often unequal pay.

(c) Women workers often suffer sexual harassment in recruitment and employment.

(d) Women workers in South Africa lose their jobs when they become pregnant also after they have to work under harmful conditions to themselves and their unborn children.

(e) Domestic workers do not have days off, in fact, no rights at all.

RESOLVES TO FIGHT:

(i) Against all unequal and discriminatory treatment of women at work and in society.

(ii) For the equal right of women and men to paid work as an important part of the aim, to achieve full and freely chosen employment.

(iii) Equal pay for all work of equal value.

(iv) To fight for the inclusion of domestic and farm workers in the labour laws of this country, like other sectors in the labour field.

(v) For child care and family facilities.

(vi) For full maternity rights, including paid maternity and job security.

(vii) Protection of women from all types of exploitation.

(viii) Protection against sexual harassment.

4 Living Conditions

We demand:

(i) Houses which enable us to live as human beings with our own human dignity.

(ii) Playgrounds, creches and nursery schools for our children.

(iii) Improvement of public transport and bus fares.

(iv) Abolition of general sales tax.

5 Programme of Action

(a) *Education*:

The present education system in our country is designed to maintain the oppressed and the exploited masses of our country in ideological bondage.

The present education system is designed to continue and reinforce the values of human dignity and to promote bosses and madams.

The education must serve the interest of the vast majority of our country.

Therefore we resolved:

(i) To establish a national, regional and local education programme for the domestic workers and farm workers.

(ii) To expose the type of education which is forced upon our children without our participation in planning the future of our children.

(iii) To develop skills and abilities so that they can manage to live on their own.

(iv) To be made aware politically.

(v) To establish national coordinating education committees locally and regionally.

(vi) To commemorate the important events and resistant days made by our mothers in our country and the general struggle wage by our people in this country.

(vii) May Day should be seen as a paid holiday.

(b) *Affiliation*:

(i) SADWU should affiliate to COSATU as soon as possible.

(ii) SADWU should be made famous even internationally by affiliating to the international bodies that carry the workers' struggle at heart.

(c) *Political Status*:

(i) 1987 should be declared 'The year of Domestic Workers' with assistance of other progressive organisations.

(ii) An immediate preparation of seminars and workshops in order to educate the workers about COSATU and other political bodies.

(iii) The present government and employers should meet our previous demands before the first day of May and, if not, domestic workers will stage a national protest.

(iv) We fully support sanctions.

(v) We also fully support NECC (National Education Crisis Committee).

Bibliography

I. Published sources including books, journal articles, pamphlets and newspapers
II. Unpublished sources
III. Official reports

I. Published sources

Abortion Reform Action Group Newsletters.

Adams, C. and Laurekietis, R., *The Gender Trap; a closer look at sex roles.* Virago, London, 1976.

Adamson, O., *et al.* 'Women's oppression under Capitalism', RCG Publications Ltd. no. 5, 1976.

Althusser, L., *For Marx.* Allen Lane, The Penguin Press, London, 1970.

Althusser, L. and Balibar, E., *Reading Capital.* New Left Books, London, 1970.

Althusser L. *Lenin, Philosophy and Other Essays.* New Left Books, London, 1971.

Andreski, S., 'Reflections on the South African Social Order from a Comparative Viewpoint' in Adam H. (ed.), *South Africa, Sociological Perspectives.* Oxford University Press, Oxford, 1971.

Anon., *Belinda's Book for Colonial Housewives.* Robinson & Co., Durban, 1916.

Ashley, M., 'African Education and Society in the nineteenth century Eastern Cape' in Saunders, C. and Derricourt, R., *Beyond the Cape Frontier. Studies in the History of the Transkei and Ciskei.* Longmans, Cape Town, 1974.

Barrett, J., *et. al., South African Women Speak.* CIIR, London. 1985.

Barrow, J., *Travels into the Interior of Southern Africa.* T. Cadell & W. Davies, London, 1806.

Beechey, V., 'Some Notes on Female Wage Labour in Capitalist Production', *Capital and Class*, 3 Autumn 1977.

Bell, C. and Newby, H., 'Husbands and Wives, the dynamics of the differential dialectic' in Barker, D.L. and Allen, S., *Dependence and Exploitation in Work and Marriage*. Longmans, London, 1976.

Bennett, A., *Riceyman Steps*. Cassell, London, 1959 edition.

Bennett, A., *Clayhanger*. Methuen & Co. Ltd., London, 1910, 1967.

Bennett, A., *The Old Wives Tale*. Hodder & Stoughton Ltd., London, 1948.

Benson, M., *The African Patriots*. Faber & Faber, London, 1963.

Bernstein, H., *For their Triumphs and their Tears*. International Defence and Aid Fund, London, 1975.

Blackstone, T. 'The Education of Girls Today' in Mitchell, J. and Oakley, A. (eds.), *The Rights and Wrongs of Women*. Penguin Books, Harmondsworth, 1976.

Bott, E. *Family and Social Network*. Tavistock, London, 1964.

Boserup, E., *Women's Role in Economic Development*. St. Martins Press, New York, 1970.

Bottomore, T.B., *Classes in Modern Society*. George Allen & Unwin Ltd., London, 1966.

Bowker, J.M. *Speeches, Letters and Selections from Important Papers of the late John Mitford Bowker*. Godlonton & Richards, Grahamstown, 1874.

Branca, P., *Women in Europe since 1750*. Croom Helm, London, 1972.

Broverman *et al.*, 'Sex Role Stereotypes: a current appraisal'. *Journal of Social Issues*. vol. 23, no. 2, 1972.

Bullock, J.B. (ed.), *Peddie: Settlers Outpost*. Grocott & Sherry, Grahamstown, 1960.

Bundy, C., 'The Emergence and Decline of a South African Peasantry', *African Affairs*. vol. 71, no. 285, 1972.

Burnett, J., *Useful Toil: autobiographies of working people from the 1820s to the 1920s*. Penguin, Harmondsworth, 1977.

Butler, G. (ed.), *The 1820 Settlers. An illustrated commentary*. Human & Rousseau, Cape Town, 1974.

Byrne, D. *et al.*, *The Poverty of Education: a study in the politics of opportunity*. Martin Robertson, London, 1975.

S.G.B. 'Life at the Cape' in *The Cape Monthly Magazine*. vol. 1, 1870.

Cairns, H.A., *Prelude to Imperialism. British reactions to Central African Society 1840–1890*. Routledge & Kegan Paul, London, 1965.

Calderwood, H., *Caffres and Caffre Missions: with preliminary chapters on the Cape Colony as a field for emigration, and basis of missionary operations*. James Nisbet & Co., London, 1858.

Callinicos, L., 'Domesticating Workers'. *South African Labour Bulletin*. vol. 2, no. 4, 1975.

Cambridge History of the British Empire. vol. II. Cambridge University Press, 1929.

Campbell, 'Latin and the Elite Tradition in Education', *British Journal of Sociology*. vol. XIX, no. 3, 1968.

Carnegie Commission, *The Poor White Problem in South Africa*. Pro-Ecclesia Drukkery, Stellenbosch, 1932.

Chase, J.C., *The Cape of Good Hope and the Eastern Province of Algoa Bay*. C. Struik (Pty) Ltd., Cape Town, 1843.

Christian Express.

Clark, K., *Animals and Men*. Thames & Hudson, London 1977.

Cock, J., *Maids and Madams: a study in the politics of exploitation*. Ravan Press, Johannesburg, 1980.

Cock, J., 'Keeping the Fires Burning: Militarisation and the politics of gender in South Africa', *South African Sociological Review*, vol. 1. no. 1, 1988.

Cock, J., Emden, E., and Klugman, B., *Childcare and the Working Mother: an urban African Study*. Carnegie Commission, Cape Town, 1983.

Conference of Socialist Economists, *On the Political Economy of Women*. C.S.E. Pamphlet no. 2, undated.

Cory, G., *The Rise of South Africa*. Longmans, London, 1910–1930. 5 vols.

Coser, L., *Greedy Institutions*. The Free Press, New York, 1974.

Daily Dispatch.

Davenport, T.R.H., *South Africa – a Modern History*. Macmillan South Africa (Publishers), Johannesburg, 1977.

Davidoff, L., 'The Rationalization of Housework' in Barker D.L. and Allen S., *Dependence and Exploitation in Work and Marriage*. Longmans, London, 1976.

Davidoff, L., *The Best Circles. Society, Etiquette and the Season*. Croom Helm, London, 1973.

Davies, R., 'The White working class in South Africa', *New Left Review*. no. 82, November-December 1973.

Davis, A., *Women, Race and Class*. The Women's Press, London, 1982.

De Beauvoir, S., *The Second Sex*. Penguin, Harmondsworth, 1976.

Deckard, B., *The Women's Movement, political, socio-economic and psychological issues*. Harper & Row, New York, 1975.

De Kiewiet, C., *A History of South Africa, Social and Economic*. Oxford University Press, London, 1957.

Delamont, S. and Duffin, L., *The Nineteenth Century Woman. Her Cultural and Physical World*. Croom Helm, London, 1978.

Dennis, N. *et al.*, *Coal is our Life: an analysis of a Yorkshire mining community*. Tavistock, London, 1969.

Desmond, C., *The Discarded People*. Penguin, Harmondsworth, 1969.

De Vos, P.J. *et al.*, *A socio-economic and educational survey of the Bantu residing in the Victoria East, Middledrift and Zwelitsha areas of the Ciskei*. Fort Hare University, 1970.

Dickason, G.B., *Irish Settlers to the Cape; a history of the Clanwilliam 1820 Settlers from Cork harbour*. A.A. Balkema, Cape Town, 1973.

Dodd, A.D., *Native Vocational Training*. The Lovedale Press, Lovedale, 1938.

Douglas, J., *The Home and the School*. MacGibbon & Kee, London, 1969.

Du Bois, W.E.B., *Darkwater. Voices from within the veil*. Constable, London, 1920.

Dunbar, J., *The Early Victorian Woman, some aspects of her life*. Harrap, London, 1953.

Duncan, S., 'The Central Institution of South African Labour Exploitation', *South African Labour Bulletin*. vol. 3, no. 9, November 1977.

Durkheim, E., *The Division of Labour*. The Free Press, Glencoe, Illinois, 1949.

Eastern Province Herald.

Edwards, I., *The 1820 Settlers in South Africa. A study in British Colonial Policy*. Longmans, Green & Co., London, 1934.

Ekwensi, C., *Jagua Nana*. Hutchinson, London, 1961.

Eliot, G., *The Mill on the Floss*. Blackwood, Edinburgh, n.d.

Evans-Pritchard, E.E. *The Position of Women in Primitive Societies and other essays in Social Anthropology*. Faber & Faber Ltd., London, 1965.

Figes, E., *Patriarchal Attitudes: Women in Society*. Faber & Faber, London, 1970.

Financial Mail.

Firestone, S., *The Dialectic of Sex*. Paladin, London, 1972.

Fisher, F., 'Class consciousness among colonised workers in South Africa' in Schlemmer, L. and Webster, E., *Change, Reform and Economic Growth in South Africa*. Ravan Press, Johannesburg, 1978.

First, R., Steele, J., Gurney, C., *The South African Connection: western investment in apartheid*. Penguin, Harmondsworth, 1973.

Forbes, V. (ed.), G. Thompson, *Travels and Adventures in Southern Africa*. Van Riebeeck Society, Cape Town, 1968.

Fraser, D., *The Teaching of Healthcraft to African Women*. Longmans, London, 1932.

From Women.

Gardiner, J., 'Domestic Labour in Capitalist Society' in Barker, D.L. and Allen, S., *Dependence and Exploitation in Work and Marriage*. Longmans, London, 1976.

Gardiner, J., 'Women's Domestic Labour', *New Left Review*. no. 89, 1975.

Garment Worker.

Garson, N.G., 'English-speaking South Africans and the British connection 1820–1961' in De Villiers, A. (ed.), *English-speaking South Africa Today: proceedings of the National Conference*. Oxford University Press, Cape Town, 1976.

Gaskill, E., *Cranford*. Dent, London, 1948.

Gavron, H., *The Captive Wife*. Penguin, Harmondsworth, 1973.

Genovese, E., 'Legacy of Slavery and Roots of Black Nationalism' in Weinstein, J. and Eakins, D.(eds.), *For a New America*. Vintage Books, New York, 1970.

Genovese, E., *The World the Slaveholders Made*. Vintage Books, New York, 1971.

George, D., *London Life in the Eighteenth Century*. Kegan Paul, Trench, Trubner & Co. Ltd., London, 1925.

Giddens, A., *The Class Structure of the Advanced Societies*. Hutchinson & Co., London, 1974.

Giddens, A., *New Rules of Sociological Method*. Hutchinson, London, 1976.

Goffman, E., *Asylums*. Penguin, Harmondsworth, 1968.

Goode, W.J. and Hatt, P.K., *Methods in Social Research*. McGraw-Hill, New York, 1957.

Gordon, S., *Domestic Workers – A guide for employers*. SAIRR, Johannesburg, 1978.

Gould-Davies, E., *The First Sex*. J.M. Dent & Sons Ltd., London, 1973.

Graham's Town Journal.

Grest, J., *African Wages in Grahamstown*. SAIRR, Johannesburg, 1974.

Grocott's Daily Mail.

Gutsche, T., *The Bishop's Lady*. Howard Timmins, Cape Town, 1970.

Hammond, D. and Jablow, A., *The Africa That Never Was. Four centuries of British writing about Africa*. Twayne Publishers, New York, 1970.

Hammond-Tooke, W.D., *Bhaca Society*. Oxford University Press, Cape Town, 1962.

Halsey, A.H., Reith Lecture no. 3. *The Listener*, 26.1.1978.

Halsey, A.H. *Educational Priority: reports of a Research Project*. HMSO, London, 1972.

Hargreaves, D., *Social Relations in Secondary Schools*. Routledge & Kegan Paul, London, 1966.

Hattersley, A., *An Illustrated Social History of South Africa*. A.A. Balkema, Cape Town, 1969.

Hill, G., *Women in English Life, from Mediaeval to Modern Times*. Bentley, London, 1869. 2 vols.

Hindess, B., and Hirst, P., *Pre-Capitalist Modes of Production*. Routledge & Kegan Paul, London 1975.

Hobson, D., 'Housewives' Isolation as Oppression', Women's Studies Group, *Women Take Issue*, Hutchinson, London, 1978.

Horn, P., *The Rise and Fall of the Victorian Servant*. Gill & Macmillan Ltd., Dublin, 1975.

Horrell, M., *The Rights of African Women: some suggested reforms*. SAIRR, Johannesburg, 1975.

Houghton, D. and Walton, E., 'The Economy of a Native Reserve', *Keiskammahoek Rural Survey*. vol. 2. Shuter & Shooter, Pietermaritzburg, 1932.

H.S.R.C., 'Female Potential'. *Newsletter* no. 103, August, 1978.

Huggett, F.E., *Life Below Stairs, domestic servants in England from Victorian Times*. John Murray, London, 1977.

Hunter, M., 'The Effects of Contact with Europeans on the Status of Pondo Women', *Africa*, vol. VI, 1933.

Hunter, M., *Reaction to Conquest. Effects of Contact with Europeans on the Pondo of South Africa*. Oxford University Press, London, 1936. Second edition, 1961.

Illich, I., *Deschooling Society*. Harper & Row, New York, 1971.

Inglis, A., *The White Women's Protection Ordinance. Sexual Anxiety and Politics in Papua*. Sussex University Press, 1975.

James, S. and dalla Costa, M., *The Power of Women and the Subversion of the Community*. Falling Wall Press, Bristol, 1973.

Johnson, R., 'Notes on the schooling of the English working class

1780–1850' in Dale, R. *et al.*, *Schooling and Capitalism*. A Sociological Reader. Open University, 1976.

Johnstone, F., 'White Prosperity and White Supremacy in South Africa Today', *African Affairs*, vol. 69, no. 275, April, 1970.

Johnstone, F., *Class, Race and Gold: a study of class relations and racial discrimination in South Africa*. Routledge & Kegan Paul, London, 1976.

Katzman, D. *Seven Days a Week. Women and Domestic Service in Industrialising America*. Oxford University Press, New York, 1978.

Keddie, N., 'Classroom Knowledge' in Young, M. (ed.), *Knowledge and Control*. Collier-Macmillan, London, 1971.

Keppel-Jones, A. (ed.) *Philipps, 1820 Settler. His Letters*. Shuter & Shooter, Pietermaritzburg, 1960.

Kitson Clark, G., *An Expanding Society. Britain 1830–1900*. Cambridge University Press, 1967.

Kitteringham, J., 'Country work girls in nineteenth century England' in Samuel, R., *Village Life and Labour*. Routledge & Kegan Paul, London, 1975.

Kuhn A. and Wolpe A.M. *Feminism and Materialism. Women and Modes of Production*. Routledge and Kegan Paul, London, 1978.

Laslett, P., *Family Life and Illicit Love in Earlier Generations*. Cambridge University Press, 1977.

Laslett, P., *The World We Have Lost*. Methuen, London, 1965.

Lawton, L., *Working Women*. Ravan Press, Johannesburg, 1985.

Leftwich, A., 'The Constitution and Continuity of South African Inequality: some conceptual considerations' in Leftwich, A. (ed.), *South Africa: Economic Growth and Political Change*. Allison & Busby, London, 1974.

Legassick, M., 'The dynamics of modernization in South Africa', *Journal of African History*, 1972, XIII, 1.

Lichtenstein, H., *Travels in Southern Africa*. Reprint. Van Riebeeck Society, Cape Town, 1928.

Little, K., *African Women in Towns: an aspect of Africa's social revolution*. Cambridge Universtiy Press, 1973.

Lockwood, D., 'Sources of variation in working class images of society', *The Sociological Review*. vol. 14, no. 3, Novermber, 1966.

Lombroso, C. and Ferrero, W., *The Female Offender*. T. Fisher Unwin, London, 1895.

Long, U., *An Index to authors of unofficial privately-owned manuscripts relating to the history of South Africa, 1812–20*. Lund Humphries, London, 1947.

Long, U. (ed.), *The Chronicle of Jeremiah Goldswain: Albany Settler of 1820*. Van Riebeeck Society, Cape Town, 1946–49. 2 vols.

Loram, C., *The Education of the South African Native*. Longmans, Green & Co., London, 1971.

Lupton, M.L., 'The Legal Disabilities of Zulu Women'. *Reality*, November, 1975.

MacCrone, I.D. *Race Attitudes in South Africa*. Oxford University Press, Oxford, 1937.

Macmillan, W.M., *Bantu, Boer and Briton, the making of the South African Native Problem*. Clarendon Press, Oxford, 1963.

Macmillan, W.M., *The Cape Colour Question: a historical survey*. Faber & Gwyer, London, 1927.

Macmillan, W.M., *Economic Conditions in a non-industrial South African Town*. Grocott & Sherry, Grahamstown, 1915.

Macpherson, C.B., 'Servants and Labourers in Eighteenth Century England' in Macpherson, C.B., *Democratic Theory: Essays in Retrieval*. Clarendon Press, Oxford, 1973.

Madge, J., *The Tools of Social Science*. Longmans, London, 1965.

Majeke, N., *The Role of the Missionaries in Conquest*. Society of Young Africa, Johannesburg, 1952.

Malherbe, E.G., *Education in South Africa. 1923–1975*. vol II. Juta & Co., Cape Town, 1977.

Marais, J.S., *The Cape Coloured People, 1652–1937*. Witwatersrand University Press, Johannesburg, 1968.

Marks, P., 'Femininity in the classroom: an account of changing attitudes' in Mitchell, J. and Oakley, A. (eds.), *The Rights and Wrongs of Women*. Penguin, Harmondsworth, 1976.

Marx, K., *Grundrisse, Foundations of the Critique of Political Economy*. Trans. with Foreword by M. Nicolaus. Penguin, Harmondsworth, 1973.

Marx, K., *Wage-Labour and Capital*. Lawrence & Wishart, London, 1933.

Marx, K., *Capital* vol. I. Penguin, Harmondsworth, 1976.

Marx, K., *Wage-Labour and Capital*. International Publishers, New York, 1971.

Mauss, M., *The Gift*. Cohen & West, London, 1970.

Maxwell, W.A., *Reconsiderations*. 1970 First Dugmore Memorial Lecture. 1820 Settlers Monument Foundation, Grahamstown, 1971.

Maxwell, W.A., and McGeogh, R.T., *The Reminiscences of Thomas Stubbs*. Balkema, Cape Town, 1978.

Mayer, P., *Townsmen or Tribesmen. Conservatism and the Process of Urbanisation in a South African City.* Oxford University Press, Cape Town, 1961.

Mbilinyi, M., 'Education, Stratification and Sexism in Tanzania: Policy Implications', *The African Review*, vol. 3, no. 2, 1973.

Mbilinyi, M., 'The New Woman and Traditional Norms in Tanzania', *The Journal of Modern African Studies*, 10,1,1972.

McLellan, D., *Marx.* Fontana, London, 1975.

Meer, F. (ed.), *Black Women. Durban 1975.* University of Natal, Durban, 1975.

Memmi, A., *The Colonizer and the Colonized.* Souvenir Press, London, 1974.

Merriman, H.J., *The Cape Journals of Archdeacon H.J. Merriman, 1848–55.* The Van Riebeeck Society, Cape Town, 1952.

Miller, K., *Sexual Politics.* Avon Books, New York, 1971.

Mitchell, J., *Women's Estate.* Penguin, Harmondsworth, 1976.

Moodie, D., *The Record on a Series of Official Papers relative to the condition and treatment of the Native tribes of South Africa.* Balkema, Cape Town, 1909.

Morse-Jones, E., *The Lower Albany Chronicle.* 5 vols. Lower Albany Historical Society, Port Alfred, 1968.

Moser, C.A., *Survey Methods in Social Investigation.* Heinemann, London, 1958.

Mphahlele, E., *In Corner B.* East African Publishing House, Nairobi, 1967.

Mphahlele, E., *The African Image.* Faber & Faber, London, 1962.

Mvubelo, L., 'Women in Industry', *South African Outlook.* vol. 110, no. 1257, February, 1976.

Newby, H., *The Deferential Worker: a study of Farm Workers in East Anglia.* Allen Lane, Penguin Books, London, 1977.

Oakley, A., *The Sociology of Housework.* Martin Robertson, London, 1974.

Oakley, A., *Housewife.* Penguin, Harmondsworth, 1976.

Pateman, T. (ed.), *Counter Course.* Penguin, Harmondsworth, 1972.

Perry, A., *African Secondary School Leavers.* SAIRR, Johannesburg, 1975.

Philip, J., *Researches in South Africa.* James Duncan, London, 1828.

Pollack, O., *The Criminality of Women.* University of Pennsylvania Press, Philadelphia, 1950.

Poulantzas, N., 'On Social Classes', *New Left Review*, no. 78, March–April, 1973.

Powell, M., *Below Stairs*. Pan Books, London, 1970.

Preston-Whyte, E.M., 'The making of a Townswoman. The Process and Dilemma of Rural-Urban Migration amongst African women in Southern Natal', *Papers from the First Congress of the Association for Sociologists in Southern Africa*. University of Natal, Durban, 1973.

Pringle, T., *Narrative of a Residence in South Africa*. Edward Moxon, London, 1835.

Rainier, M. (ed.)., *The Journals of Sophia Pigot*. Balkema, Cape Town, 1974.

Ralls, A.M., *Glory which is yours. A tribute to pioneer ancestors*. Shuter & Shooter, Pietermaritzburg, undated.

Rand Daily Mail.

Renier, G.J, *History: its purpose and method*. Allen & Unwin, London, 1950.

Rex, J., *Race, Colonialism and the City*. Routledge & Kegan Paul, London, 1973.

Rex, J., *Race Relations in Sociological Theory*. Weidenfeld & Nicolson, London, 1970.

Rex, J., 'The Plural Society: the South African Case', *Race*, vol. XII, no. 4, April, 1971.

Rivett-Carnac, D., *Thus Came the English in 1820*. Howard Timmins, Cape Town, 1961.

Roberts, M., *Farm Labour in the Eastern Cape*. SAIRR, Johannesburg, 1959.

Rosenthal, R.L. and Jacobson, L., *Pygmalion in the Classroom: Teacher Expectation and Pupils' Intellectual Development*. Holt, Rinehart & Winston, New York, 1968.

Ross, B.J., *Brownlee J. Ross: his ancestry and some writings*. Lovedale Press, Lovedale, 1948.

Roux, M. and St. Leger, M., *Grahamstown's Fingo Village*. SAIRR, Johannesburg, 1971.

Rowbotham, S., *Hidden from History: 300 years of women's oppression and the fight against it*. Pluto Press, London, 1973.

Rowbotham, S., *Women's Consciousness, Man's World*. Penguin, Harmondsworth, 1973.

Rubin, G., 'The Traffic in Women: Note on the "Political Economy of Sex" ' in Reiter, R. (ed.), *Towards an Anthropology of Women*. Monthly Review, Press, New York, 1975.

Ruskin, J., *Sesame and Lilies*. George Allen & Unwin Ltd., London, 1868.

Sachs, E.S., *Rebel Daughters*. McGibbon & Kee, London, 1957.

SAIRR, *Survey of Race Relations*, 1974, 1977, 1978, SAIRR, Johannesburg.

Samuel, R. (ed.), *Village Life and Labour*. Routledge & Kegan Paul Ltd., London, 1975.

Savage, M., 'The Political Economy of Health in South Africa', *South African Outlook*, vol. 108, no. 1288, October 1978.

Savage, M., 'Costs of enforcing apartheid and problems of change', *African Affairs*, vol, 76, no. 304, July 1977.

Scharf, B., 'Sexual Stratification and Social Stratification', *British Journal of Sociology*, vol. 28, no. 4, December 1977.

Schreiner, O., *Women and Labour*. T. Fisher Unwin, London, 1911.

Schutz, A., *The Phenomenology of the Social World*. Heinemann, London, 1972.

Schutz, A., *Collected Papers*. 3 vols. Martinus Nijhoff, The Hague, 1962, 1964, 1966.

Secombe, W., *The Housewife and her Labour under Capitalism*. Socialist Woman Special. I.M.G. Publications, Second edition, 1974.

Seidman, A., 'The Economics of Eliminating Rural Poverty' in Palmer, R. and Parsons, N., *The Roots of Rural Poverty in Central and Southern Africa*. Heinemann, London, 1977.

Sell and Johnson, 'Income and Occupational Differences between Men and Women in the United States', *Sociology and Social Research*, vol. 62, no. 1, October 1977.

Sellditz, C. *et al.*, *Research Methods in Social Relations*. Revised one-volume edition. Henry Holt & Co., New York, 1959.

Sharp, R. and Green, A., *Education and Social Control: a study in progressive primary education*. Routledge & Kegan Paul, London, 1975.

Shaw, W., *The Story of my Mission in South Eastern Africa*. Hamilton, Adams & Co., London, 1860.

Shepherd, R. *Lovedale, South Africa. The Story of a Century*. Lovedale Press, Lovedale, 1940.

Shepherd, R., *Bantu Literature and Life*. Lovedale Press, Lovedale, 1955.

Shrew. Children's Books Issue. vol. 5, no. 4, October 1973.

Simons, H.J., *The Legal Status of African Women*. C. Hurst & Co., London, 1968.

Skota, T., *African Yearly Register*. R.L. Esson & Co., Johannesburg, 1931.

Smart, C., *Women, Crime and Criminology*. Routledge & Kegan Paul, London, 1977.

Smith, E.W., *The Blessed Missionaries*. Oxford University Press, Cape Town, 1950.

Soga, J.H., *The Ama-Xhosa: Life and Customs*. Lovedale Press, Lovedale, 1931.

Solomon, B., *Time Remembered. The Story of a Fight*. Howard Timmins, Cape Town, 1968.

South African Labour Bulletin.

Stewart, J., *Xhosa Phrase Book and Vocabulary*. The Lovedale Press, Lovedale, 1899, 1976.

Stirk, D., *Southwell Settlers*. Southwell, the author, 1971.

Stone, C., 'Industrialization and Female Labour Force Participation', *South African Labour Bulletin*, vol. 2, no. 4, 1976.

Stone, L., *The Family, Sex and Marriage in England, 1500-1800*. Weidenfeld & Nicolson, London, 1977.

Streek, F. (ed.), *Domestic Servants.*. A study of the service condition of domestic servants employed by Border members of the Black Sash and South African Institute of Race Relations. Black Sash, Beacon Bay, 1974.

Stuart, J. and Malcolm, D. (eds.), Fynn, L., *The Diary of Henry Francis Fynn*. Shuter & Shooter, Pietermaritzburg, 1950.

Sunday Times.

Terkel, S., *Working*. Penguin, Harmondsworth, 1977.

Theal, G.M., *Records of the Cape Colony*. vol. XXV. Government of the Cape Colony 1897-1904.

Thomas, T., *Their Doctor Speaks*. Mary Wheeldon, Cape Town, 1973.

Thompson, R., *Lark Rise to Candleford*. Oxford University Press, London, 1973.

Tomalin, C., *The Life and Death of Mary Wollstonecraft*. Penguin Books, Harmondsworth, 1977.

Treiman, D. and Terrell, K., 'Women, Work and Wages – trends in the female occupational structure' in Land, K.C. and Spilerman, S., (eds.), *Social Indicator Models*. Russell Sage Foundation, New York, 1975.

Van Allen, J., 'Sitting on a man: colonialism and the lost political institutions of Ibo women', *Canadian Journal of African Studies*, VI, II, 1972.

Van der Vyver, *Seven Lectures on Human Rights*. Juta & Co., Cape Town, 1976.

Vietzen, S., *A History of Education for European Girls in Natal with particular reference to the establishment of some leading schools, 1837-1902*. University of Natal Press, Pietermaritzburg, 1973.

Walvin, J., *Black and White, a study of the Negro in English society from 1555 to 1945*. Allen Lane, London, 1973.

Wandor, M. (ed.), *The Body Politic*. Stage 1, London, 1972.

Ward, H., *The Cape and the Kaffirs: a diary of 5 years residence in Kaffirland*. Henry G. Bohn, London, 1851.

Weinrich, A.K., 'Social Stratification and change among African women in a Rhodesian Provincial Town' in ASSA Sociology Southern Africa, 1973. Papers from the First Congress of the Association for Sociologists in Southern Africa. University of Natal, Durban, 1973.

Weinrich, A.K., *Mucheke: race, status and politics in a Rhodesian community*. UNESCO, Paris, 1976.

Welsh, D., 'English-speaking whites and the racial problem' in De Villiers, A. (ed.), *English-speaking South Africa Today. Proceeding of the National Conference, July 1974*. Oxford University Press, Cape Town, 1971.

Welsh, D., 'The Growth of Towns' in Wilson & Thompson, 1971.

Wessels, D., 'Manpower Requirements and the utilisation of women: the view of 50 employers in nine major industry groups'. Institute for Manpower Research, H.S.R.C., 1975. MM-25.

Westergaard, J. and Resler, H., *Class in a Capitalist Society. A study of Contemporary Britain*. Heinemann, London, 1976.

Westmore, J. and Townsend, P., 'African women workers in the Textile Industry in Durban', *South African Labour Bulletin*, vol. 2, no. 4, 1975.

Whisson, M.G. and Weil, W.M., *Domestic Servants: A Microcosm of the Race Problem*. SAIRR, Johannesburg, 1971.

Whiteside, J., *History of the Wesleyan Methodist Church of South Africa*. Elliott Stock, London, 1906.

Williams, D., *When Races Meet*. The life and times of William Ritchie Thomson, Glasgow Society Missionary, Government Agent and Dutch Reformed Church Minister, 1794–1891. A.P.B. Publishers, Johannesburg, 1967.

Williams, N.A., 'Just a little stretch of road', *Staffrider*. vol. 1, no. 4, November–December 1978.

Williams, R., 'Base and Superstructure', *New Left Review*, no. 82, November–December 1973.

Wilson, F. *et al.*, *Farm Labour in South Africa*. David Phillip, Cape Town, 1977.

Wilson, F. and Perrot, D. (eds.), *Outlook on a Century, 1870–1970*. SPROCAS, Lovedale Press, Lovedale, 1973.

Wilson, F., 'An Assessment of the English-speaking South Africans' Contribution to the Economy – Another point of view' in De Villiers, (1976).

Wilson, F., Migrant Labour in South Africa. SPROCAS, Johannesburg, 1972.

Wilson, M., The Interpreters. Third Dugmore Memorial Lecture. 1820 Settlers Monument Foundation, Grahamstown, 1972.

Wilson, M. and Thompson, L. (eds.), The Oxford History of South Africa. vol. I South Africa to 1870. Clarendon Press, Oxford, 1969. vol. II. South Africa 1870–1966. Clarendon Press, Oxford, 1971.

Wilson, M., The changing status of African women. Bertha Solomon Memorial Lecture. National Council of Women, Cape Town, 1974.

Wilson, M. and Mafeje, A., Langa. A study of social groups in an African township. Oxford University Press, Cape Town, 1963.

Wilson, M., 'Co-operation and Conflict on the Eastern Cape Frontier' in Wilson, M. and Thompson, L., The Oxford History of South Africa. vol. I Oxford Universtity Press, Oxford, 1969.

Wolpe, A.M., 'The Offical Ideology of Education for Girls' in Flude, M. and Ahier, J. (eds.), Educability, Schools and Ideology. Croom Helm, London, 1974.

Wolpe, H., 'The white working class in South Africa', Economy and Society. vol. 5, no. 2, 1976.

Wolpe, H., 'Capitalism and cheap labour-power in South Africa: from segregation to apartheid, Economy and Society. vol I, no. 4, Autumn, 1972.

'Women in Action', Woman power.

Woolf, V. A Room of One's Own. Penguin, Harmondsworth, 1962.

Wright, H., The Burden of the Present: Liberal-Radical Controversy over South African History. David Phillip, Cape Town, 1977.

Writers and Readers Publishing Co-operative, Sexism in Children's Books, 1976.

Wyn, B., 'Domestic subjects and the sexual division of labour' in Open University, E202 School Knowledge and Social Control. Open University, London, 1977.

Young, G.M. (ed.), Early Victorian England 1830–1865. 2 vols. Oxford University Press, London, 1934.

Young, M., 'An Approach to the study of Curricula as socially organised knowledge' in Young, M., Knowledge and Control. Routledge & Kegan Paul, London, 1971.

Young, R., African Wastes Reclaimed. The Story of the Lovedale Mission. J.M. Dent, London, 1902.

Young, S., 'Fertility and Famine: women's agricultural history in Southern Mozambique' in Palmer, R. and Parsons, N. (eds.), *The Roots of Rural Poverty in Central and Southern Africa*. Heinemann, London, 1977.

Zeitlin, I., *Rethinking Sociology*. Appleton-Century-Crofts, New York, 1973.

II. Unpublished sources

(a) *Manuscripts*

Charles Bell Diary. MS. 7287 Cory Library for Historical Research.

The Harman Papers. MS. 14773–5 Cory Library for Historical Research,

Hottentots Contract of Hiring and Service in Albany 6/2/1841. MS. 2219 Cory Library for Historical Research.

Letters from George and Anne Impey. MS. 866. Cory Library for Historical Researh.

Letters from George Impey. MS. 869. Cory Library for Historical Research.

Mary Moffat's Journal. MS. 6027 Cory Library for Historical Research.

Philipps Papers, vol. 5. MS. 7612 Cory Library for Historical Research.

Philipps Letters. MS. 14264 Cory Library for Historical Research.

Thomas Shone Diaries. MS. 10548; MS. 10763–5 Cory Library for Historical Research.

Joseph Stirk's Journals. MS. 7334 Cory Library for Historical Research.

Mrs Mary Taylor's Journal. MS. 15613 Methodist Archives, Cory Library for Historical Research.

(b) *Theses and Papers*

Antrobus, G., 'Farm Labour in the Eastern Cape 1950–1973.' Unpublished paper, August 1976.

Donaldson, M., 'The Council of Advice at the Cape of Good Hope 1825–1834. A study in colonial government.' Ph. D. thesis, Rhodes University, 1974.

Edgecombe, R., 'The Letters of Hannah Dennison 1820 Settler 1820–1847.' M.A. thesis, Rhodes University, 1968.

Fihla, P., 'The Development of Bantu Education at the St. Matthews

Mission Station, Keiskamma Hoek, 1853–1959.' M. Ed. thesis, University of South Africa, 1962.

Getz, A., 'A Survey of Black Wages in the Grahamstown Area. May 1976–1977.' Unpublished Research Project, Rhodes University, 1978.

Hewson, L., 'Healdtown, a study of a Methodist experiment in African education.' Ph. D. thesis, Rhodes University, 1959.

Lacey, M., 'Land, Labour and African Affairs, 1924–34.' M.A. Thesis, Rhodes University, 1979.

Mayer, I., Grahamstown. Unpublished Research Project, 1979.

McGeogh, R.T., 'The Reminiscences of Thomas Stubbs: 1820–1877.' M.A. thesis, Rhodes University, 1965.

Moyer, R.A., 'A History of the Mfengu of the Eastern Cape 1815–1865.'SOAS. Ph. D. thesis, 1976.

Nyquist, T.E., African Middle Class Elite. Unpublished Research Project, I.S.E.R., Grahamstown, 1969–70.

Peires, J.B., 'A History of the Xhosa, c. 1700–1835.' Unpublished M.A. thesis, Rhodes University, 1976.

Preston-Whyte, E.M. 'Between Two Worlds. A study of the working life, social ties and interpersonal relationship of African women migrants in domestic service in Durban.' Unpublished Ph.D. thesis, University of Natal, 1969.

Preston-Whyte, E.M., 'Race Attitudes and Behaviour. The case of domestic employment in white South African homes.' Paper delivered at the Sixth Annual Congress of A.S.S.A., Durban, 1975.

Rich, P., 'Ideology in a Plural Society: the case of South African segregation.' Paper delivered at A.S.S.A. Conference, Swaziland, June/July 1975.

Sack, G.D. 'The Anthropology of Development in the Ciskei.' Paper delivered at the I.S.E.R. 'Workshop on the Ciskei', Grahamstown, June 1977.

Slee, A., 'Some Aspects of Wesleyan Methodism in the Albany District between 1830 and 1844.' M.A. thesis, University of South Africa, 1946.

Study Group on Women in Employment, 'Memorandum on Women in Employment.' February 1978.

Walker, C., 'Suffrage and Passes – Two South African Women's Campaigns.' Paper presented at the Women's Seminar, Stutterheim, September, 1975.

Walther, M., 'Patterns of Life in Domestic Service'. Unpublished Honours thesis, University of the Witwaterstrand, 1968.

Williams, D., 'The Missionaries on the Eastern Frontier of the Cape Colony 1979–1853.' 2 vols. Ph.D. thesis, University of the Witwatersrand, 1959.

Willsworth, M. 'Transcending the Culture of Poverty in a Black South African Township.' M.A. thesis, Rhodes University, 1979.

III. Official Reports

Blue book, 27/1977.

C.A.C.O 5967. Blue Book, 1825. Population Returns.

Cape of Good Hope Blue Book. Educational Return for 1840. C.A.

Cape of Good Hope Blue Book. Educational Return for 1853. C.A.

Cape of Good Hope Annexures 1864/1. Report of the Superintendent-General of Education on the Industrial Institutions and Schools.

Cape of Good Hope Annexures 1881/1. Report of the Superintendent-General of Education for the year ending 30 June 1880.

Cape of Good Hope Annexures 1881/1. Superintendent-General's Report.

Cape of Good Hope 1891 Census.

Cape of Good Hope Annexures 1907/1. Report of the Superintendent-General of Education for the year ending 30 September 1906.

Census of the European Population, 1926. U.G. Union of South Africa Blue Books, 22–31, 1930.

C.O. 51/15 A.5. Copy of the Register kept in the district of Albany of contracts for service executed from 4/7 to 3/12/1828 between inhabitants of the Colony and Caffres or other foreigners under the provision of Ordinance 49. Cape Archives.

Departmental Commission on Native Education. Superintendent-General's Report. 1919.

Department of Bantu Education. Annual Report, 1967.

Parliamentary Papers 1835, XXXIX(50).

Population Census 1970, Nature of Education. Report No. 02–05–02 Republic of South Africa Department of Statistics, 1975.

Population Census 1970. Occupations. Report No. 02–05–04. Pretoria: The Government Printer, 1975.

Statistics of House and Domestic Servants. Report no. 11–03–12. Pretoria: The Government Printer, 1976.

Index

Ruth First and Ann Scott
Olive Schreiner

A Biography

'The good things about this book are so numerous that I shall
return to it again and again for information and illumination ...
I have read few books from which I have learned so much'
Phyllis Grosskurth, *Observer*

Born in 1855 in the Cape Colony, Olive Schreiner, writer, sexual
radical and champion of African rights in South Africa, is one of
the great precursors of modern feminism. She is best
remembered for her influential novel *The Story of an African Farm*,
although *Woman and Labour* (1911) became a central text of the
women's movement.

Ruth First and Ann Scott's work was quickly established as the
definitive biography of Olive Schreiner and is a major
contribution to feminist biographical writing.

Ruth First, author of *117 Days*, was a South African political
activist and journalist. She was assassinated by forces of the
apartheid regime in Maputo in 1982. Ann Scott is a feminist
writer and critic. Her new book on women psychoanalysts is
to be published by The Women's Press.

Biography   Illustrated   £6.95
ISBN: 0 7043 4156 5

Shula Marks, Editor
Not Either an Experimental Doll

Between 1949 and 1951 three very different South African
women entered into a painful and revealing correspondence,
which was to change their lives.

Lily Moya, a young Xhosa girl, desperate to escape the life
dictated to her by a racist state, writes to Mabel Palmer, a 'liberal'
British expatriate, working in the 'non European' section of the
University of Natal. Lily hopes that she can gain educational
guidance and friendship from Mabel Palmer. Sibusisiwe Makhanya,
one of the first Black social workers in South Africa, tries to act
as a mediator between these two women; but what emerges
from these letters is a series of misunderstandings caused by
cultural ignorance, racism and the fear in whites of having any
true, free and equal dialogue with a Black person.

Here we have a first hand account of the roots of modern
Apartheid and the hated Black education system.

The letters speak for themselves, but Shula Marks has written an
explanatory introduction and epilogue, which tells us of the tragic
ending to this riveting story.

Memoirs/Women's Studies   £5.95
ISBN: 0 7043 4048 8